A GUIDE TO
PUBLIC SPEAKING

A GUIDE TO PUBLIC SPEAKING

WILLIAM STEDMAN
Bucks County Community College

Prentice-Hall, Inc.
Englewood Cliffs, New Jersey

© 1971 by Prentice-Hall, Inc.
Englewood Cliffs, N.J.

Current printing (last number):
10 9 8 7 6 5 4 3 2 1

P 13–370635–4
C 13–370643–5

Library of Congress Catalog Card No.: 70–136283

Printed in the United States of America

Contents

creating interest; Focusing on the subject quickly; Using the
illustrative story to do so; Advice on humor; Wit versus joke;
Previewing the speech; Salutation.

4. **Unfolding Your Tent   29**

Approaches in presenting the body of a speech; Organizational patterns: chronological, spatial, comparison and contrast, divisional, logical; Reasons for selecting or combining
various patterns.

5. **What's the Point?   42**

Common neglect of the conclusion; Its importance; Need for
more than summary; Devices: statement of thesis, prediction,
quotation, illustration, statement of personal intention, challenge; Phrases to avoid; After the talk: the question period.

SUPPORTING MATERIAL

6. **Words in Support   57**

Factual support in a speech; Use of opinion: individual and
public; Support through rhetorical devices: definition, description, rhetorical comparison (simile, metaphor, analogy),
the illustration; Suggestions for telling a story; Repetition and
restatement as rhetorical devices.

7. **"Let Me Illustrate"   79**

The reasons for using visual aids; Basic kinds of aids: models,
graphics, charts-tables-graphs, chalk and display boards,
optical devices; Techniques of presentation; Do's and don'ts.

PRESENTATION

8. **The Delivery   105**

Delivery as a means of enhancing communication; Disadvantages of memorization; Advantages of extemporaneous
method; Using notes that help; Reading from a manuscript;

Mechanical problems of reading; Marking the manuscript; Housing and handling the pages.

Word selection: naturalness, avoidance of jargon, simplicity; Waste words; Pronunciation; Exercises.

SPECIAL SPEECHES

The inclusiveness of the speech to persuade; Knowing the idea and the audience; Reaching and motivating listeners through appropriate channels; Presenting the idea intelligently and fairly (with special reference to errors in reasoning and flaws in presentation); Using an organizational pattern appropriate to audience's perception of the issue; Actuation; Review.

The speech of introduction; The speech of presentation; The speech of response; Speeches of tribute: testimonial, memorial, eulogy; A note on style.

APPENDICES

A GUIDE TO
PUBLIC SPEAKING

ORIENTATION

chapter 1

Unaccustomed as I Am

We don't know how it began—this taken-for-granted thing we call speech—but back on the dark side of time, begin it did. And how fully we human beings have used it through the centuries!

We have used it to rally armies, instruct our children, remember our dead, earn our livings, and order our groceries. The words of our mouths have produced fear, hate, tears, laughter, and downright boredom.

Most of the time we speak to one another in small groups, comprising perhaps no more than two people. This we call conversation. For most of us it's easy. But to almost everyone comes that time when conversation will not do, that time when we are required to undertake a project which for most of us seems anything but easy. We have to make a speech.

Why do we do it? Often it's to *explain or describe* something to an interested, or even an uninterested, group. We also make speeches to *meet a special situation,* or to *tell a story,* or possibly to *sell a thing or an idea.* Sometimes a speech is designed to do nothing more than *entertain.*

Not many of us make speeches specifically to entertain. That is the province of the professional. But sooner or later we encounter the other speech situations. We have to tell our associates at work how a new plan or process works. We speak up at a rally concerning the pollution or wasting of our natural resources. We are called upon to introduce a guest speaker or to present the athlete-of-the-year award. Perhaps we try to convince the folks at the monthly town meeting that it's wrong to censor movies or to keep certain books off the library shelves.

We might do all these things, or things very much like them. Such obligations go hand-in-hand with leadership, or advanced education, or concern for the world about us. Fortunately, with a little training and experience, we can transform these challenges into worthwhile experiences—for both our audience and ourselves. Who knows? We might even enjoy it.

How is it possible to enjoy something that scares you half to death?

That's a good question. For some reason, a dozen or so people whom you don't mind at all talking to individually take on the aspect of a body of inquisitors when you face them collectively. Joe or Harry or Carol or Ann are great people when you're standing beside them, yet when you're standing before them and they're looking at you, wondering what you're going to say, you wish you could slip through the crack in the floor. Failing that, the building might catch on fire. That would let you escape making the speech. But how many buildings catch on fire when someone is speaking—despite the superabundance at times of wind to fan the flames? Instead of engaging in wishful thinking, then, why not learn how to cut your stage fright to a minimum so that it doesn't interfere with the business at hand?

It can be done. After all, the problem is not yours alone. Nervousness before an audience is found in almost everyone, from rank beginner to experienced professional. George Cukor, the motion-picture director who won an Academy Award for *My Fair Lady*, likes to tell the story of a famous actress and singer who is stricken with terror before every performance or production number. Cukor could never understand this because, when the singer played the Palladium in London, people stood on chairs to applaud her performance.

"With all your success, why the stage fright?" he asked her.

"It's easy," she answered. "I always figure that this is the time they're going to get me."

Well, as Cukor puts it, "they never have, and they never will." But it's quite possible that the butterflies the lady feels in her stomach give her just enough extra adrenalin to bring about a top-notch performance. It is well to keep in mind that a little nervousness is a good thing. Speakers who don't feel nervous are speakers who drone on for what seems like hours, never saying much worth hearing and never knowing when to stop. They feel no pain. Only their audience does.

Recognizing that a bit of nervousness is both natural and desirable, what can you, as a speaker, do to keep your uneasiness from getting out of hand? First of all, you can *prepare well* for the task ahead. Nothing matches the feeling of confidence that is yours if you know you're on top of the subject. Good football teams have that feeling before a big game. They know they have practiced hard and have done their homework thoroughly. They are ready for whatever comes.

I am not suggesting that you must study and practice as long for a speech as a football team does for a game—though it has been done. I am suggesting, however, that a minute spent in looking up the pronunciation of a word such as "apartheid" can pay dividends when you come to that part of your speech in which you have to use it. Perhaps you are going to introduce a guest speaker. Why not try to learn something about him before the day you give your remarks. When you rise to attack or defend a controversial idea such as capital punishment, surely you will feel more comfortable if you have investigated the problem enough to know whereof you speak. Then too, nothing helps more than giving a touch of organization to your thoughts—forming them into the familiar introduction, body, and conclusion.

Chances are that as you get ready for your speaking assignment, the subject itself will grow more interesting. Subjects that seem dull at first often are much more promising after you get beneath the surface. If you find yourself getting enthusiastic about your topic, you will also find that *enthusiasm* begins displacing fear. The speaker who is captured by his subject doesn't have much time to worry about what will happen to him after he takes the platform.

Remember that most of the things a beginning speaker worries about don't happen at all. Audiences, when you think about it, are simply collections of people much like the speaker himself. Ordinarily, they're not a bad sort. They don't usually boo, or throw vegetables, or walk out of the auditorium. About the worst they'll do during the average speech is look a trifle bored—which is their privilege if the speaker hasn't tried to interest them.

So when you face an audience, *hold good thoughts for the people in it.* Maybe they're the same Joe and Harry and Carol and Ann that you enjoy talking with at other times. Even if they're strangers, they're still people. Generate some warmth toward them and they will return it to you. Those good thoughts you hold will chop away at stage fright just as enthusiasm does.

One more bit of advice to reduce tension. *Don't rush things.* You would be surprised how many speakers hurry to the rostrum and, in their haste to get the job over with, start to speak before their breathing mechanisms are working normally. Take a few seconds to get ready. Put your notes in a good position on the stand. Many professional speakers relax in just this way. Look at your audience to let the people know you are aware of them. And when everyone seems comfortably settled yourself included, start to speak.

Your comfort will be greater, I might add, if you *don't worry about your hands.* If you wish, rest them lightly on the lectern. Or leave them at your sides; it may feel unnatural, but it looks perfectly all right. If you do feel a gesture coming on, make it. Natural gestures look much better than contrived ones. And, gentlemen, forget about putting one hand in the side pocket of your coat—unless you wish to look like a banker in a 1935 movie. In fact, it's a good idea to avoid putting your hands anywhere except on the speaker's stand. That means not in pockets, not on the hips, not on the belt, not on the kidneys, not on the biceps, not on the lapel, not on any of the apparently endless parts of the attire or anatomy you've seen speakers discover as places to rest fingers or hands. If there's no lectern on which to rest your notes, you may wish to hold—but not clutch—them at your side or at waist level. It's better than sneaking them in and out of your coat pocket.

What I am really saying is, "Use common sense, suppress the urge to do something fancy and, hard as it may appear, *try to be yourself.*" Sooner or later you will realize that naturalness rubs off on an audience. You will also realize that your hearers, if you afford them a fair chance, will be more interested in what you have to say than in what you look or sound like.

For the moment, then, let's not worry about stage fright or techniques of delivery. Let's see if we can give the audience a speech worth listening to.

chapter 2

Is This Speech Necessary?

We're joking, of course, when we ask if a speech is necessary. More than a few speeches are made for ample reason without being, in a strict sense, necessary. Nevertheless it's a good idea, when sitting down to prepare a talk, to ask yourself, "Why am I making this speech?"

Now you can toss aside your query by answering, "Because my professor requires it," or "Because the boss told me I had to." But that's begging the question. Remember, it was, "Why am I making *this* speech?" not "Why am I making *a* speech?" What are the things that distinguish your talk from others that might be made on the same general subject? What distinguishes it from one you might make on that subject at another time—or to a different audience?

In other words, *what is your objective* in terms of this audience at this time? When you're all finished, what do you hope you have imparted to those who heard you? Why did you use the words you did, show the visual aids you showed, ask the rhetorical questions you asked? Why did you make this speech?

The "why"—your objective—is really much more needful of consideration than your subject. If you are taking a speech course you will obviously have to devise speech topics to meet stated assignments

"Now that we've learned to talk, try to speak the same language."

or guidelines of your instructor. Consider this a good opportunity for exercising creative imagination. Beyond the classroom, however, the subject is normally there waiting for you: a Selective Service plan, the United Fund drive, the union's salary demands, the proposed changes in the zoning laws. It will be in the handling, not the selection, of the subject that you will have the greatest freedom of movement.

If, as you plan your speech, you spend a little time thinking about why you are making it, your presentation will be vastly more effective. Do you wish simply to talk in broad terms about the new constitution of your organization or do you wish to show how much simpler and more effective it is than the old one? Will you be content with saying a few nice words about skiing or do you hope to attract your classmates to the ski club? In more brutal terms, are you going to come through to the audience as a wishy-washy dispenser of miscellaneous and disconnected information or as someone who knows what is to be said and says it?

Setting down your specific purpose, your objective, is the first step in achieving it. Everything grows from this base. After all, if you, the speaker, don't have clearly in mind what you intend to do, how can you expect your audience to find any point to your remarks?

Oh, you could go before your hearers and say anything that comes to mind about your subject. That is exactly how a good many speeches are made, without an objective and without preparation. Or you could study everything at hand about the topic and then cut loose. That was the pulpit technique of the old-time preacher who advised: "'Read yourself full; think yourself clear; pray yourself hot; then let yourself go!" Although there is preparation of a sort in this procedure, there is little certainty of reaching the goal—if one ever appears amid the verbiage.

To make any real progress you have to look squarely at your subject and your reason for talking about it. This holds true for a highly controversial subject or one that is commonplace. Whether it be drug usage or the duck-billed platypus, you have to have a point of view.

To demonstrate, let's select a thoroughly innocuous topic—one to which few of us would bring already fixed viewpoints that could get in the way of the illustration. Let's suppose that you have been asked to talk to the Young Homemakers Club on the subject of soup. (Stay with us, please!) Now, if you were a public-relations representative of the soup industry, your objective probably would not be hard to isolate. No doubt you would be out *to build goodwill for your product, packaged soups.* And of course, if you were a representative of the Apex Soup Company, you would want to go further than that; you would try *to get your audience to buy soup, specifically Apex.* Objectives such as these are not too difficult to pinpoint because they fall within the general area of persuasion.

When you have to deliver an information speech, however, objectives do not spring forth so clearly. You have to do a little more thinking—particularly with a less-than-dramatic subject, such as soup.

Still, recognizing the limitations of the topic can be an important part of distilling the objective. It's doubtful that you could say anything truly startling about soup—that eating a bowl a day can cause hair to grow on bald heads, for example. So you might as well set aside any thought of rocking the listeners back in their seats. From a broad viewpoint, soup is soup.

Well then, could you attempt something within the area of possibility? Could you, for instance, tell your audience that soup tastes good?

You might. To set out to tell your audience that soup tastes good is an objective, something on which a speech could be built. But would it be worth it? Suppose you did hold forth the flavor delights of the savory liquid, would anyone really care? And would they have had any different thoughts about it in the first place, or learn anything new? The soup-tastes-good objective is a good example of purpose without much point. Only the gifted essayist could do much with it, on paper or on a speaker's platform.

Would it be possible, you might ask, to upgrade the objective a bit? Instead of concentrating upon the palate-pleasing qualities of your topic, could you assert that soup is a worthwhile food? This might be a little better. A highly motivated elementary-school audience might find such information acceptable payment for the time spent in listening to your brief. It's doubtful, though, that any other audience would. Once again, the fulfillment of the objective is hardly worth the effort.

Is there anything, then, that you can do with the subject of soup to stir a ripple of interest in a mature audience? Possibly there is, if you stop to think about that audience. You are going to speak to the Young Homemakers, remember. And what are most young homemakers interested in? Saving money, for one thing—or, more precisely, making ends meet. Why not tie your speech to this never-ending problem of the younger couple? Why not let your objective be *to show that soup is one of the best food bargains?*

Now you have a case worth demonstrating. You could show that soup is high in nutritional content, that it costs very little per serving, that few foods can match it in cost per vitamin, that there is a low-priced, nourishing soup to appeal to almost every taste, and so on. From a matter-of-fact, unbiased point of view you would be showing your specific audience a way to hold on to some precious pennies.

That the soup salesman would be delighted with your remarks

is incidental; your over-all purpose remains to inform. You are not attempting to uphold a special interest by whatever ethical means available, as the salesman would be. You are simply presenting a reasoned point of view within a framework of objectivity. Were soup not a good food buy, it would become your obligation to say so. The salesman, on the other hand, would avoid a negative aspect or attempt to discount it in some way. His interest is persuasion; yours, information.

SPECIAL CONSIDERATIONS

Not all topics are as free of controversy as the one we've been using in our hypothetical address to the Young Homemakers. Moreover, different audiences will react in different ways to the same subject. Even our seemingly harmless objective in the soup speech might prove inappropriate to certain groups. Try to tell some Pacific Islanders who live quite pleasantly and inexpensively on wild fruits and wild boar that soup is their best food bargain and you're likely to be drowned in laughter. Try it on a group of cannibals and you're likely to be part of the bargain.

When the subject is controversial, the possible audience reactions are manifold. Would you talk to an over-40 audience about teen-age driving in exactly the same way you would to the teen-agers themselves? Of course not. No more than you would talk about the need for a wage increase in the same way to the board of directors and those on the picket line.

Obviously, not all audiences are as distinguishable as those we've just mentioned. Yet that is all the more reason to think carefully about the make-up of that group of individuals which will gather to hear you. Are they what is loosely called a "homogeneous" group? If so, what are the characteristics of age, income, education, or sex that draw them together? And if the individuals are basically dissimilar, what factor or factors unify them for the moment? A holiday or special tribute? An interest in ecology, or birds, or sports cars, or football? Any gaps in your knowledge of the audience when you begin assembling your speech should be filled as soon as possible.[1]

Don't end your analysis with audience composition. Give some

[1] Audience analysis, particularly as it pertains to persuasion, is examined in greater detail in Chapter Ten.

"By George, son, do you realize what we are doing? We are communicating."

attention to the psychological factors that can influence your reception. Is your speech to be given early in the morning, late in the afternoon, or after dinner? Audience response will vary with the degree of fatigue. Don't expect to accomplish as much with a group that can't wait to get home to dinner as you would with one that has just dined and is ready to sit back and do some listening.

Also, take note of your place on the program. Are you the first speaker, the last speaker, the only speaker? This could affect what you plan to say. If you are last on the program, the audience could be too weary of speechmaking to be initially receptive to you. You will have to work hard on your opening remarks. By way of compensation, however, the last speaker has the last word—and often he doesn't have to waste time on preliminary details his predecessors have been assigned to cover. He can refine his objective that much more.

In reality, no place on the program is in itself good or bad.

Nonetheless, knowing your moment in the spotlight can help you plan your attack. Once again we come to the question: What is your objective in terms of this audience at this time? "Time," here, can mean time of year, time of week, time of day, time on program. It can even mean time on stage, for certainly you can't expect to accomplish in a three-minute speech what you would in one lasting thirty minutes.

Setting or narrowing the objective of your speech is largely a matter of common sense and discipline. Common sense will help you with audience analysis and the selection of an objective if you exert just enough discipline to make yourself answer "Why am I making this speech to this audience at this time?"

One last suggestion about this: To nail down your objective, try capturing the essence of it in a single sentence. If you can, not only will you have produced the delight of English and speech teachers, *a thesis*, you will have so pinpointed your efforts that there will be no danger of your audience wondering what you were talking about— even if you don't actually state the thesis in the speech itself.

When you leave things at "I'm going to tell my audience about the growing problem of air pollution," you are being comfortably vague—and you can expect a corresponding reaction from your audience. But set out to support and build upon the thesis:

> Air pollution is a danger to the health of every person in this community—not twenty years from now, but now.

—and you will produce an outline with force behind it. Your audience, whether sympathetic to your position or not, will know at least that you have taken one.

FROM SUBJECT TO THESIS

At this point it might occur to you to ask, "How can I always know enough about my subject at the beginning to work out a precise objective—let alone a thesis sentence?" If you are wondering about this, you're on good ground. In many instances you simply can't take the step of setting down the exact objective until you've done a little work. It all depends upon the subject.

For instance, if you are concerned about the way your classmates or fellow workers are abusing their school or office building, you know right away what the broad goal of your speech is: to get your associates to respect and take care of their 9-to-5 quarters. Refining the objective and stating the thesis wouldn't be difficult because most of the problem would lie within your experience. This doesn't mean that you would work out the whole speech by sitting in an easy chair with a notepad on your knee, but it does mean that some topics are more adaptable to direct analysis than are others.

The honor system, for example, is a bit too complicated for quick resolution in an informative speech. It's easy enough to say, on the basis of whatever knowledge you have, "I'm for it," or "I'm against it"—but what if you have been asked by the student government of Mainstreet College to present an introductory report on the subject, without prejudice one way or the other? Obviously, you would have to do a little research to move your objective beyond a somewhat loose statement such as: "to explain to the student government how the honor system works at some American colleges and universities."

Beyond doubt, beginning with this broad statement which can be narrowed is infinitely superior to simply planning to talk about the honor system. But before starting on the actual speech it is advisable to do some investigating. Keeping in mind the purpose of the talk and the audience for which it is intended, you begin to gather basic material.

At the library you check the card catalog for books on education that trace the history and workings of honor systems. A little background reading—supplemented by some note-taking, of course—can soon put you on comfortable footing with your subject. While at the library don't forget the pamphlet file, or the *Readers' Guide to Periodical Literature,* which allows you to look at what the more recent magazines are saying about the subject. And take advantage of the other guides and directories that are available at the library to help you find the information you need on this or any other subject.

Not all research materials rest in the library, however. A subject such as the honor system gains new dimensions all the time. What do the people not writing books and magazines think about it? If it's functioning at a neighboring college, perhaps it will be possible for you to visit the campus and see it in action. If the nearest observation point is too far away for that, maybe a letter to the student government will get results. People are usually flattered by inquiries of this kind, and like to comply.

And don't forget the people at home. Almost every college or high-school faculty contains one or two instructors who taught or studied at a school where some form of honor system was in effect. Your reading, followed by a look at the faculty roster in the local college catalog, will tell you which instructors to talk with. Find out what they learned about the honor system from direct experience. See how they think it might be utilized at Mainstreet College. Talk also with the Mainstreet students. What would they think of trying the honor system? How well do they think it would work?

Now, clearly you may not have time to do all these things. Still, you should try to collect as much material as you can to bridge the gap between your broad preliminary objective and a refined thesis sentence. Perhaps, in the instance I've been using, your narrowed objective would be to demonstrate, with appropriate background material, how an honor system might function at Mainstreet College. This might lead to a thesis such as, "If Mainstreet College were to adopt an honor system, Variation X is one plan that might be used." Your hypothetical explanation of Variation X at Mainstreet would give the audience an excellent take-off point for analysis, discussion, and further investigation.

Other subjects, needless to say, can be taken from broad objective to thesis sentence in much the same way—through reading, inquiring, observing. As you must recognize, the information you gather for this purpose is the same information you will draw upon for the speech itself. As often as not, you need do no more collecting. Your objective-refining efforts, therefore, really serve a double purpose. With your notecards already before you, you can start to outline your speech.

A LOOK AHEAD

In the next three chapters you will find suggestions that should help you develop the broad pattern and approach of an outline. For your convenience the chapter sequence is that of the speech itself: introduction, body, conclusion. Naturally, you will often prepare the introduction after fashioning the body—and you may begin your preparations with a concluding statement in mind. Our chapter arrangement should not, therefore, be taken as an indication of priority, though it does present the material in the order in which it is heard by the people in your audience.

As to the exact format your outline should take, we must give precedence to the wishes of your instructor or to a technique you may have acquired in earlier instruction and found to be effective. If you require further guidelines, however, an outline form is presented at the end of this book. In Chapter Four that form is used in a sentence outline.

ORGANIZATION AND STRUCTURE

chapter 3

Beginning

The first words you speak are important. From them your listeners will form an impression that probably will last throughout the speech. Your task is to make that impression a favorable one. If you fail in this, the whole presentation might wind up a pointless exercise in rhetoric.

Considering the importance of the introduction, it's surprising that it is so often abused, even by experienced speakers. More potentially interesting speeches are ruined by bad beginnings than we could total in a lifetime. In some ways it's easier to set forth the rules for quickly losing an audience than it is to give the ones for gaining one.

For example, to get the audience to stop caring right away, tell them in your first sentence that you doubt if they'll be interested in what you have to say. This works every time. A nice negative attitude on your part will make your listeners think, "If he doesn't think I'll be interested, why is he so determined to bore me with what he has on his mind?"

Should expressing uncertainty about audience interest not appeal to you as a way of losing attention, try telling your hearers that the subject is too complicated to be explained or that you don't really know how to begin such a complex undertaking. Instantly your listeners will begin to wonder why you are bothering at all, and will let their thoughts stray to a subject more susceptible to analysis, such as the big party coming up on the weekend.

And—bad rule number three—attach insult to injury by blaming the whole problem on the audience:

> This is a somewhat difficult subject. You might not understand.

Just a little condescension on your part can turn a trusting audience into a sullen body of sorely offended souls. There is nothing like talking down to people as a way of closing their minds and ears.

Now we're sure that you would never fall into one of these audience-losing traps—but we're equally sure that you've been the victim of them in the speeches of others. To give you a little extra assistance in avoiding an instant loss of attention, suppose we talk about some of the things that properly belong in the opening portion of your remarks. How should you begin a speech?

First, have a positive attitude, in bearing and in expression. Let your body show that you are ready to talk about something important and let your words support this impression. Any feeling of inadequacy you might have should be cast aside before you reach the speaker's stand. To your audience, you must appear ready to provide a solid return for the minutes of their lives they are giving to you. Even when the subject is sad or unpleasant, let your listeners know you are going to give them full measure. You can show this with your posture and countenance before you open your mouth.

Second, when you do begin speaking, start strong. Have a well-formed opening. It might be a statement:

> When I was ten years old I fell in love with a woman 152 feet tall.

or a question:

> In the next twelve months how many of your friends or acquaintances will suffer or die because someone was careless?

or a few words borrowed from another:

Long ago, in another troubled era, a newcomer to America wrote, "These are the times that try men's souls."

Whatever your beginning, select it with the care that can win the attention and, it is hoped, the interest of your audience in a matter of moments.

Yet, as important as it is to gain attention quickly, I am not suggesting that you carry things to the point of out-and-out gimmickry. There are those speakers who fire blank cartridges or rip off their suit jackets and throw them at the audience to arouse interest. No question about it, they do get attention. But by and large their remarks are as enduring as the echo of the cartridge, and only the shock of their opening sticks in the minds of their listeners. The big-bang opening is a risky device that often turns the audience away from, instead of toward, a speaker. Use it only with the greatest caution and only if you can relate it instantly to the subject. Otherwise your audience will think itself in the presence of a fool or a show-off—and they might have good reason to think so.

On the other hand, don't assume it is sufficient to paraphrase William Shakespeare and ask the audience to lend you its ears. If Marc Antony had left it at that, the restless Roman assemblage would have paid him no heed. Shakespeare wisely supplied him with a salutation to put him on common ground with his skeptical audience —"Friends, Romans, countrymen"—and a follow-up sentence to calm their doubts about his purpose: "I come to bury Caesar, not to praise him." Though the Bard had the comfort of intervening centuries in preparing the speeches of his characters, I suspect that Mr. Shakespeare could have done well as a professional speechwriter if he hadn't taken up the drama.

Many centuries after that day on which Marc Antony addressed his Roman compatriots, another public official in another land spoke a word of introduction to his countrymen. His opening, with its unconventional way of numbering, is as well-known as the old Roman's fictional one. Who, when pretending to deliver an oration, cannot draw a full breath and repeat:

> Fourscore and seven years ago our fathers brought forth on this continent a new nation, conceived in liberty and dedicated to the proposition that all men are created equal.

That oft-recited first sentence of the Gettysburg Address is so familiar that we sometimes fail to notice how well Abraham Lincoln used his second one to bring a seemingly innocuous, if not overblown, opening line into dramatic perspective. In two dozen words he vividly portrayed the situation of this country in 1863:

> Now we are engaged in a great civil war, testing whether that nation or any nation so conceived and so dedicated can long endure.

It is no wonder that Edward Everett, the famous orator who also spoke that day at Gettysburg, wrote Lincoln, "I should be glad if I could flatter myself that I came as near the central idea of the occasion in two hours as you did in two minutes." [1] Everett, the experienced platform performer, recognized that the President had the whole of his well-received speech in focus at the end of two sentences.

Obviously, we cannot expect to achieve the style and eloquence of Abraham Lincoln—or of Marc Antony's ghostwriter. But we can take note of what they did in their memorable introductions. And that was to pose the problem rapidly, without bothering with the fanciness so many speakers feel compelled to tack on to their openings.

We, like they, have to look for those good opening words that make the listener say, "Aha! This is going to be worth hearing."

One of the most effective introductory lines this writer ever heard was in question form and was delivered by a student. The chap perked up a somewhat lethargic group of apprentice speakers with the line:

> Have you ever been cursed by a 300-pound Gypsy woman?

Needless to say, his classmates listened carefully to what followed that interest-building opening. Nor were they disappointed by what they heard, for his beginning was not just a trick but, as it turned out, an integral part of his presentation.

That's the trouble with so many of the stories speakers use at the outset of their talks. They're artificial. The speaker says something like this:

> Looking at this array of earnest faces, I am reminded of a story.

Then he reels out a shopworn tale that too often has nothing at all to do with those earnest faces. He is reminded of the story only because

---

[1] P. R. Frothingham, *Edward Everett, Orator and Statesman* (Boston: Houghton Mifflin Company, 1925), p. 458.

it is the one he uses to begin all his speeches, whatever the subject, whatever the audience and occasion. This fellow would be far better off if somehow that venerable story at last slipped from his mind.

Not that telling a story is a bad way of beginning a speech. It must have bearing on the moment, that's all. Here is one that advertising man Bruce Barton used both to generate interest in his subject and to help show his audience the value of advertising regularly. It concerned a promotional man who worked for a circus:

> It was his function to precede the circus into various communities, distribute tickets to the editor, put up on the barns pictures of the bearded lady and the man-eating snakes, and finally to get in touch with the proprietor of some store and persuade him to purchase the space on either side of the elephant for his advertisement in the parade.

> Coming one day to a crossroads town our friend found that there was only one store. The proprietor did not receive him enthusiastically. "Why should I advertise?" he demanded. "I have been here for twenty years. There isn't a man, woman or child around these parts that doesn't know where I am and what I sell." The advertising man answered very promptly (because in our business if we hesitate we are lost), and he said to the proprietor, pointing across the street, "What is that building over there?" The proprietor answered, "That is the Methodist Episcopal Church." The advertising man said, "How long has that been there?" The proprietor said, "Oh, I don't know; seventy-five years probably." "And yet," exclaimed the advertising man, "they ring the church bell every Sunday morning." [2]

Barton's story clearly made a point. And he followed it with another analogy—that of Joseph in the Bible—to amplify the point: Just as a Pharaoh of later years knew not Joseph or what he had done to save Egypt from famine, babies born at the moment Barton was speaking knew not that Ivory soap floated. They would have to be told. That is why, as Barton explained subsequently in his speech, good public relations was a "very constant business," one on which Ivory's maker was willing to spend a million or more dollars each year.

Bruce Barton's stories were so well selected he could spend the

2 Bruce Barton, "Which Knew Not Joseph," in *Modern Speeches,* comp. Homer D. Lindgren (New York: Crofts, 1930), p. 358.

rest of his speech building upon them. They were not artificial additions designed to drag in a bit of humor; they were essential ingredients of his remarks. They belonged. The circus tale might even have drawn a chuckle or two from his audience. Certainly it was more entertaining than the leaden tales speakers so often "are reminded of."

USING HUMOR IN THE INTRODUCTION

I don't wish to imply that it's wrong to capture an audience—and possibly get them interested in your topic—with an amusing anecdote or humorous story. But it is dangerous to unroll what is obviously Anecdote No. 9H in your portfolio, especially if you're not a skilled raconteur. Telling a joke is an art few people acquire. If you are one of the gifted, fine. If not, try to let your humor grow out of the occasion, the subject matter, or some natural part of the situation.

A fine use of humor—and one that tied the address to the occasion—was displayed in a peacetime reunion of the British veterans of El Alamein. Viscount Bernard Montgomery, the commanding general in that important battle of 1942, moved onto a dramatically lighted auditorium stage a quarter-century later to speak to the men who had served under him. Emotion was so great by the time he appeared that Montgomery could merely have uttered a few "pip-pip's" and some platitudes and then basked in the glow of respect that had accumulated around the old soldier in twenty-five years. He chose instead to emphasize his human, not his heroic, side.

The retired field marshal told his veterans that he had received a letter which, judging from the handwriting, had come from a nine-year-old boy. Here is what the lad wrote:

> Dear Sir:
> I thought you were dead.
> My father says that you are not, but that you will die soon.
> Please send me your autograph—quickly.

The warm laughter that dotted Montgomery's reading of the note from a young admirer both revealed and tightened the bond of affection between speaker and audience.

Montgomery, in directing the humor toward himself, was once again sharing an experience with his men, that of growing old. Further, he was emphasizing that while the hand of time touches both general and foot soldier, that touch can erase former distinctions of rank and station, making all, at a moment of reunion, of one mind and heart. Viscount Montgomery delivered his anecdote in excellent fashion, but his recognition of the usefulness of the letter for the specific situation of the reunion was more important than his delivery. Using it was a matter of ingenuity or, if you wish, wit.

Wit, surprisingly enough, can be fashioned by most speakers after a little practice and is often appreciated more than the precooked joke. It seems spontaneous, and frequently is. An audience feels that a quip or a piece of business such as Montgomery's letter was designed for it alone. Even an old joke can be effective if it's dressed up for the situation and appears fresh. Here again, ingenuity—what you do with a story or bit of self-history—will carry you farther than a book of 1,000 gags for all occasions.

The only occasion you're interested in is the one for which you are preparing your speech. It is doubtful that the author of any joke book anticipated it exactly, no matter how much you pay for the volume of well-worn pleasantries. If you can turn an old chestnut into something that's right for the moment, well and good; if not, better forget the idea. Be alert to the possibility of slipping a smile or two into your introduction, but don't regard it as a matter of life or death to do so.

More often than not, the opportunity for some laughter pops up naturally as you prepare your talk. There are many things from which it can come—the occupation of most of your audience, the special interest that pulls them together, the reputation that has preceded you, the little-known and unimportant anniversary on which your speech happens to fall, the group that's meeting in the adjoining room, and so on. As you size up the audience and occasion, take note of the elements that might lend themselves to lightness, then see what develops. Just don't try to force things.

To be perfectly honest, your best opportunity for adding humor to your introduction may come in those minutes during which you are waiting to give it. It may stem from the remarks of those preceding you on the program, or from the kind of day it has turned out to be, or from some completely unanticipated occurrence. In planning your opening, recognize that you must be prepared for the unexpected.

President Kennedy, in fact, let the things that preceded his remarks provide a sure path to the winning of an audience. He listened carefully to what others said before he spoke, jotting down ideas for rejoinders that invariably delighted the crowd. A potential disaster, such as a collapsing microphone, usually provoked from him a comment that brought both laughter and sympathy from his hearers. He was never too dignified to take note of the little things we all enjoy chuckling at. Mr. Kennedy struck many blows at the pomposity that constantly creeps into speechmaking, and at the same time he made those blows serve him most effectively in capturing the interest and respect of his listeners. We would do well to follow his example.

PREVIEWING

So far we have seen how a good opening sentence or two, or perhaps a story, can gain attention and lead the audience into your subject. For many purposes this will be sufficient introduction. When your purpose is essentially informative or instructional, however, it may be desirable to go a little further. Before launching into the body of the speech itself you might wish to let your audience know what you're up to. Those who have experience in the military will recognize this technique as part of the formula:

1. Tell them what you're going to tell them. (Introduction)
2. Tell them. (Body)
3. Tell them what you've told them. (Conclusion)

It all may seem a bit mechanical but, believe it or not, it usually works. Through this presentation sequence millions of young men have been introduced to a variety of skills, from camouflage to first aid, which, though of little interest to them initially, become the skills that one day may save their lives.

The human mind, it seems, needs a little time to adjust to a new or a previously unimportant topic. Most of the time we can't catch a detailed scheme on the fly and transfer it to memory. The preview, therefore, helps the audience set itself mentally for what is to come.

When you tell your audience that you are going to present the three steps in Process X and then list those steps, you are really giving your hearers a chance to focus their thoughts before it is too late. And "too late" may very well be the body of the speech, if Process X is a subject of any amount of complication. An unsignaled explanation may not be enough for perspective—or even for understanding. That is why a minute or less spent on previewing can be invaluable to your over-all presentation. It can mean the difference between getting your message across or confusing your audience with fragments of a concept.

Closely associated with previewing is the offering of background information to add meaning or understanding to the speech. The value of a new device, for example, often becomes much more apparent when the weaknesses of earlier ones are enumerated. And a bit of historical perspective will not hurt a speech on a topic unfamiliar to many in the audience—from the game of lacrosse to the Battle of Bull Run. Keep this background brief, however. It mustn't mire the speech.

THE SALUTATION

One more thing should go into this chapter: the salutation. Is it necessary to address specifically those who are gathered to hear you? Generally it is not. And in the present day, to do so can appear a bit pretentious.

Still, there are occasions when the situation or degree of formality demands some sort of "Friends, Romans, countrymen." They probably would be occasions at which you are addressing a distinguished group you do not normally encounter or one obviously containing hierarchies that are customarily recognized. An academic ceremony is a good example, as is a meeting of an important professional or scientific society.

At such occasions the normal procedure is to give the salutation in descending order of rank, keeping the number of groupings at a minimum. Thus it would be, "President Hale, members of the faculty, fellow students" or "Superintendent Bell, members of the faculty of Lincoln High, distinguished graduates, parents, and friends." The ordering of rank should reflect the moment; some might wish to mention the graduates first at a commencement exercise.

In a salutation you are extending a courtesy that can be given some kind of logical base and should be kept as simple as possible. If you name one person of a given status you must name all of that status or run the risk of offending. Hence, keep the groupings few and inclusive. This is especially true when the audience is so diversified as to invite comparison to a laundry list if all parties are enumerated. President Roosevelt may have been parodied for the "my friends" he used to introduce his fireside chats of radio, but his technique was infinitely simpler than that used by Italian dictator Benito Mussolini one day in 1940. He began his announcement of his nation's entry into World War II in this fashion:

> Fighters of land, sea and air, Blackshirts of the revolution and of the legions, men and women of Italy, of the empire and of the Kingdom of Albania, listen! [3]

There is still something to be said for the simple things.

CLOSING NOTES

In this chapter we have seen that a good introduction can do several things. It can: (1) win the attention of the audience; (2) establish rapport or a common ground between speaker and listeners; (3) create interest in the subject; and (4) preview or give background to what is to come.

Not every successful introduction will serve this quadruple function, of course. Nor will the four aspects always be divisible one from another. Nevertheless, it is not a bad idea to keep the fourfold possibilities of the introduction in mind at the outset, when the speech is planned, and to think carefully before setting aside one of the parts.

[3] Benito Mussolini, "Address of June 10, 1940," *New York Times*, June 11, 1940.

chapter 4

Unfolding Your Tent

Your introductory remarks, no matter how interesting, aren't of much value unless what follows them is worth hearing. So we shouldn't put off any longer our first look at the body of the speech.

As you probably know, several other names have been manufactured for this section of the talk, some of them quite elegant. Yet none has caught the public fancy sufficiently to replace the term "body." To avoid confusion, therefore, we'll stick with the designation most commonly used. If you wish to use another one, by all means do so. It isn't the label for the heart of the speech that's important, after all. It's what you say in it.

Like the introduction, the body of your presentation can follow several patterns, any one of which can be right if it lets you accomplish your objective. The only pattern, in fact, which is not to be relied upon for any situation is the accidental one. The depth of planning in this approach—dear to the heart of one Alfred E. Neuman of *Mad Magazine*—is aptly revealed in his famous aphorism:

What—me worry?

Without pointing to any flaw in the homely philosophy of Master Neuman, may we suggest that expecting to figure out what you will do in the body of a speech after you have delivered the introduction is like plunging into a jungle minus compass, map, or guide. Things may turn out right, but more often they won't—unless you adopt the point of view of the hungry lion into whose den you stumble. Let us not count, then, on jujus or oratorical gods to extricate us from tangled undergrowth. Instead, let's look at ways to cut through to our destination.

It is customary to assign neat designations to the several patterns for the body of a talk. The possible implication is that the speech planner will studiously flip through an imaginary pattern book, as he might an album of wallpaper samples, let his mind's eye come to rest on one possibility, and then say to himself, "Aha! I will lay out the central portion of my speech using Mode SPB407: Comparison and Contrast."

This may be the way it is for the beginning speaker (though I doubt it), but it certainly is not the way an experienced lecturer goes about things. The actual process is much more natural, much less contrived, and probably free of any labeling whatever. As we look at the different ways of unfolding a speech, please keep this in mind. These arbitrary classifications, which do not have the same names in all texts, are presented solely for your consideration in organizing your remarks. They are not absolutes. The distinctions among them are not razor-sharp. And what you call them, if anything, is of no importance once you know them.

ARRANGEMENT BY TIME

Ofttimes logic itself will suggest the path you should follow. For instance, if you were speaking on the rise of the former American Football League it would be quite natural for you to follow a chronological, or time, pattern. You could begin with the League's modest (though not inexpensive) beginning, trace its rise to a position as a real threat to the older, established football group, and finally show its position as a full partner in the destiny of professional football. Incidentally, when using the time pattern, it is a good idea to keep the divisions few —three at the outside, in a short talk. Things can get complicated if there are too many phases to remember.

Although historical and narrative speeches seem the most natural channels for the time order, other kinds of talks can benefit from this arrangement. The instructional lecture is one, especially if it is of the how-to-do-it type. Steps 1, 2, and 3 of changing a tire, for example, are really points in time. Thus, a speech that demonstrates a process is by its nature involved with time progression.

By the way, while time moves ever forward in our daily lives, it can be turned around in a speech. Don't overlook the possibility of starting with now and working back to then. You might decide to paint the picture of a present-day slum district, then by degrees take that area back to a position of former glory or even to a state of nature uncontaminated by man. Time or process reversal can add insights to a subject that would not otherwise be revealed.

ARRANGEMENT BY SPACE

Much like the chronological framework is the one based upon spatial arrangement. In this format the parts of a whole are presented one at a time, as they relate to each other. Things might run from left to right, top to bottom, inside to outside, and so on. Julius Caesar was using this technique in his *Commentaries on the Gallic War* when he began:

Gaul is divided into three parts.

A student speaker might use the same idea for a speech on the sections of a department store or the parts of an internal-combustion engine or the layers of a golf ball. The point of beginning—inside or out, top or bottom—will be important or incidental, depending upon the intent of the speaker and the subject itself. While it doesn't matter much which part of the golf ball you start with, an explanation of internal combustion would be more meaningful if the components were introduced in relationship to the operational sequence: intake, compression, power, exhaust. Just remember to have some plan, rather than a haphazard presentation of parts.

This spatial framework, I should add, can be extended to such things as administrative divisions, even though the physical relationship exists on an organizational chart. I refer to the familiar chain of command in a business organization, a military unit, or a college.

Here again, the speaker has the option of starting with the colonel and working down to the private or approaching things from bottom to top. The actual operational sequence—the flow of business, the routing of a request—might suggest at which end to begin. Ordinarily it doesn't take long to select the appropriate way.

Later on, when we come to the section on visual aids, I'll have more to say about this format.

COMPARISON AND CONTRAST

Another general pattern of organization is comparison and contrast. Actually, the designation covers two different, though related, approaches, for comparison builds upon the similarities of things placed side by side and contrast upon their differences.

This pattern doesn't need much explanation, so instead of elaborating upon the obvious, let's see how two speakers used it. First I quote a portion of a speech made by Senator George Graham Vest back in 1870. His purpose was to win a law suit for a client whose fine hunting dog had been shot by a man who suspected it of killing some of his sheep. In part, here is what Vest said in his remembered "Eulogy to the Dog":

> The best friend a man has in the world may turn against him and become his enemy. His son or daughter that he has reared with loving care may prove ungrateful. . . . The money that a man has he may lose. . . . A man's reputation may be sacrificed in a moment of ill-considered action. . . .
>
> > The one absolutely unselfish friend that a man may have in this selfish world . . . is his dog. Gentlemen of the jury, a man's dog stands by him in prosperity and poverty, in health and sickness. He will sleep on the cold ground. . . . He will kiss the hand that has no food to offer, he will lick the wounds and sores that come in encounter with the roughness of the world. He guards the sleep of his pauper master as if he were a prince. When all other friends desert he remains. When riches take wings and reputation falls to pieces he is as constant in his love as the sun in its journey through the heavens. . . . And when the last scene of all comes, and death takes the master in its embrace . . . there by the grave-

side will the noble dog be found, his head between his paws, his eyes sad but open in alert watchfulness, faithful and true even in death.[1]

Vest, through his adept use of contrast between things canine and non-canine, won the verdict for his client and resounding huzzahs from dog lovers all over the world.

Seventy-five years later another public official (who once asked his critics to attack him, not his little black Scotty, Fala) prepared a speech for delivery to the nation. President Franklin D. Roosevelt did not live to deliver the address that would have been one of his familiar fireside chats, but the unfinished talk was preserved nonetheless and is a good example of comparison of things past and present. It was to have been delivered on the eve of Thomas Jefferson's birthday, as Jefferson Day dinners were taking place around the country. Calling our third President an "American citizen of the world," Roosevelt presented three then-and-now comparisons while urging his listeners to look toward a time of peace that lay near at hand.

1. . . . Jefferson was instrumental in the establishment of the United States as a vital factor in international affairs. It was he who first sent our Navy into far distant waters to defend our rights. And the promulgation of the Monroe Doctrine was the logical development of Jefferson's far-seeing foreign policy.

   Today this Nation which Jefferson helped so greatly to build is playing a tremendous part in the battle for the rights of man all over the world. Today we are part of the vast allied force—a force composed of flesh and blood and steel and spirit—which is today destroying the makers of war, the breeders of hate, in Europe and in Asia.

2. In Jefferson's time our Navy consisted of only a handful of frigates—but that tiny Navy taught nations across the Atlantic that piracy in the Mediterranean—acts of aggression against peaceful commerce and the enslavement of their crews—was one of those things which, among neighbors, simply was not done.

---

[1] George Graham Vest, "Eulogy to the Dog." A convenient source of the surviving portion is Bower and Lucile Folse Aly, *American Short Speeches* (New York: The Macmillan Company, 1968), pp. 48-49.

Today we have learned in the agony of war that great power involves great responsibility. Today we can no more escape the consequence of German and Japanese aggression than could we avoid the consequences of attacks by the Barbary corsairs a century and a half before. We, as Americans, do not choose to deny our responsibility. . . . But the mere conquest of our enemies is not enough. We must go on to do all in our power to conquer the doubts and the fears, the ignorance and the greed, which made this horror possible.

3. Thomas Jefferson, himself a distinguished scientist, once spoke of the "brotherly spirit of science, which unites into one family all its votaries of whatever grade, and however widely dispersed throughout the different quarters of the globe."

Today, science has brought all the quarters of the globe so close together that it is impossible to isolate them one from another. Today we are faced with the pre-eminent fact that, if civilization is to survive, we must cultivate the science of human relationships— the ability of all peoples, of all kinds, to live together and work together in the same world, at peace. Let me assure you that my hand is the steadier for the work that is to be done. . . . The work, my friends, is peace. . . .[2]

At first thought it might seem that pairing of times a century-and-a-half apart would result in contrast, not comparison, but Roosevelt was of course emphasizing the enduring wisdom of Jefferson that brought the separated generations of Americans together in spirit and obligation. The idea was a good one and the never-delivered speech still stands as a piece of literature.

ARRANGEMENT THROUGH DIVISION

Often, as you prepare a speech, you will find it convenient to divide your subject into several natural categories. It can make things much easier to handle for both speaker and audience, especially if the subject is complex.

[2] Franklin Delano Roosevelt, "Undelivered Jefferson Day Address," *New York Times*, April 14, 1945. Also in *Classic Speeches*, ed. Richard Crosscup (New York: Philosophical Library, 1965), pp. 392-94.

Lyndon Johnson used this technique to introduce his concept of the Great Society:

> . . . So I want to talk to you today about three places where we begin to build the Great Society—in our cities, in our countryside, and in our classrooms. Many of you will live to see the day, perhaps fifty years from now, when there will be 400 million Americans; four-fifths of them in urban areas. . . . So in the next forty years we must rebuild the entire urban United States. . . .
>
> A second place where we begin to build the Great Society is in our countryside. . . . For once the battle is lost, once our natural splendor is destroyed, it can never be recaptured. . . .
>
> A third place to build the Great Society is in the classrooms of America. There your children's lives will be shaped. . . .[3]

Mr. Johnson selected the cities, the countryside, and the classrooms (all beginning with the letter "c") to represent the "central issues of the Great Society." Was this a use of the space pattern? Only by extension, for the three issues really were urban growth, conservation, and education. The President translated these abstract problems into physical entities to make them easier to visualize. And even before this he had to choose them as the issues on which to focus. A little imagination transformed a giant topic into workable units.

Does this mean that division is unusually challenging or difficult? Not at all. Talks on the varieties of cows, or swimming strokes, or tennis serves resolve themselves quite nicely into their basic subdivisions. And inspirational messages have a way of becoming partitioned into units such as "duty, honor, country," or "faith, hope, and charity."

With an intricate topic you are likely to go beyond simple classification. You might decide to break down the whole topic into its component parts, real or assumed:

> Let's isolate and examine the musical and electronic elements of the rock-and-roll sound.

This separation into specific elements—*analysis*—is a good technique for describing the nature of a thing, the inner relationships.

[3] Lyndon Johnson, "The Great Society," Commencement Address, University of Michigan, June, 1964. Found in *Voices in Crisis,* ed. Floyd W. Matson (New York: The Odyssey Press, Inc., 1967), pp. 111-14.

Analysis corresponds to taking a watch apart to see what makes it tick. Needless to say, it requires some forethought and knowledge of the subject, especially when it goes beyond a structure the eye or ear can readily detect and becomes the technique of logical reasoning we shall meet in a few pages.

If the analytical pattern is reversed—if you put the building blocks on top of one another instead of pulling them off—you have what is called *synthesis:*

> We're going to fashion a mosaic today and the first ingredient we need is integrity. . . .

Synthesize if you wish to stress building or assembling; analyze if you wish to move from the whole to the parts. The distinction is mainly one of emphasis.

At times the order in which divisions are presented is not immediately evident. When speakers do no more than flip a coin mentally and present areas in random fashion, the pattern is merely *enumeration.* A weak pattern, it is best used to reinforce another. Only poets have done much with it singly:

> *How do I love thee?*
> *Let me count the ways.*[4]

If, on the other hand, there's good reason for saving the most important or most touching until last, you could employ the *climactic* arrangement. The successive elements are of increasing significance till the final one is revealed. Observe how the Indian leader, Chief Joseph, arranged his moving speech of surrender.

> *Tell General Howard I know his heart. What*
> *he told me before, I have it in my heart.*
> *Our chiefs are killed.*
> > *Looking-Glass is dead.*
> > *Ta-Hool-Hool-Shute is dead.*
> > *The old men are all dead.*
> *It is the young men who say yes or no.*
> > *He who led on the young men is dead.*

---

[4] Elizabeth Barrett Browning, *Sonnets from the Portuguese.*

It is cold, and we have no blankets.
The little children are freezing to death.
My people, some of them have run away
To the hills, and have no blankets, no food.
No one knows where they are—
perhaps freezing to death.
I want to have time to look for my children
And see how many of them I can find.
Maybe I shall find them among the dead.
Hear me, my chiefs!
I am tired; my heart is sick and sad.
From where the sun now stands
I will fight no more forever.[5]

Was this mere enumeration of dead chiefs, leaderless young men, unrelieved cold, runaway people, and lost children as reasons for surrender? Or was each reason for ending warfare more compelling than the one which preceded it? Turn the elements around if you're not sure of the answer.

Occasionally the topical grouping is not confined to the content, but is extended to the audience itself. Possibly the most conspicuous example of this was President John Kennedy's Inaugural Address. Do you recall how he addressed the various segments of the national or world population, to whom in each instance he offered a specific pledge?

To those old allies . . .
To those new states whom we welcome to the ranks of the free . . .
To those people in the huts and villages of half the globe struggling to break the bonds of mass misery . . .
To our sister republics south of the border . . .
To that world assembly of sovereign states, the United Nations . . .
Finally, to those nations who would make themselves our adversary . . .

After the series of pledges, Mr. Kennedy narrowed the direction of his address to the U.S. and its Cold War opponents and, using

---

[5] Chief Joseph, "Surrender Speech," *Harper's Weekly,* November 17, 1877, p. 906. Also in Aly, *American Short Speeches,* pp. 66-67.

enumeration and the repeated phrase "Let both sides," presented another series of thoughts for improving the world situation. At the end
of the speech he skillfully merged the six groups of the earlier part
of the address into two simpler, yet more universal ones:

> And so, *my fellow Americans:* Ask not what your country can
> do for you. Ask what you can do for your country.
> *My fellow citizens of the world:* Ask not what America will do
> for you, but what together we can do for the freedom of
> man. [Italics added.]

Where might you use this technique of divided address? Well,
possibly not at your inauguration as President of the United States, but
perhaps in your induction into office in your class or organization. In
such an instance you might group your remarks as they apply to
officers past, officers present, members, and sponsors or advisors.
Farewell speeches are frequently constructed on this pattern also, as
are addresses at academic ceremonies, particularly commencements.

PATTERNS OF LOGIC

Sometimes an organizational pattern is expanded or absorbed
into a pattern of logical reasoning. Suppose you would attempt to
prove how something came about by tracing it to earlier and identifi-
able happenings or actions. This exacting analysis usually is called
cause and effect. It incorporates the chronological format, but is not
quite the same.

A speech on the sinking of the "Titanic," for instance, could
follow the time-order approach. The incidents could be recounted
as they happened without particular stress on the "why" of the disaster. On the other hand, if the speaker should, from the beginning,
attempt through a chain of evidence to attribute the great loss of life
to a series of human failings or errors, he would not be saying simply,
"This is what happened," he would be saying, "This happened because. . . ."

Suppose I set up just such a talk using this technique. Let me do
it in the form of a sentence outline—the method you might very well
use in outlining your speeches. Only the main points are set down, of
course.

Introduction

On April 14, 1912, twenty minutes before midnight, the world's largest ship, the "Titanic," struck an iceberg. Two hours and forty minutes later, the vessel that could not sink slipped under the waves, taking 1,500 passengers and crew with it. Most of these lives were lost because of human errors *before* the iceberg was struck.

Body

I. The "Titanic" received repeated warnings of icebergs in the area, but its officers ignored them.

    A. All day long the messages came in:

        1. From the "Caronia" at 9:00 A.M.

        2. From the "Baltic" at 1:42 P.M.

        3. From the "Amerika" at 1.45.

        4. From the "Californian" at 7:30.

        5. From the "Mesaba" at 9:40.

    B. At 11:00 P.M., forty minutes before the collision, the nearby "Californian" sent another warning. It was rudely received and was interrupted before the position of the bergs could be given.

    C. The collision, therefore, could have been avoided had those on the "Titanic" given greater heed to the many warnings or allowed the last one to be completed.

II. After the collision it was still possible to save the lives of most on board through standard safety procedures. The "Titanic's" operators, however, had given only lip service to such precautions.

    A. There were not enough life jackets for all.

    B. The number of lifeboats fell short of need.

    C. There had been no practice in abandoning ship. Of the boats that managed to be released, some pulled away only partly filled.

III. Even these blunders would not have taken such toll had the nearest vessel taken any part in the rescue. But the "Californian," only ten miles away, did not.

    A. The rudeness of the "Titanic's" wireless operator gave the radioman of the "Californian" little reason to stay

in touch with the nearby vessel as the two ships moved
through the icefield.

B. Wireless regulations at the time were inadequate.
Twenty-four-hour operation on passenger vessels was
not required.

C. The "Californian's" radioman, weary after a hard day,
closed down his set only ten minutes before the
"Titanic" struck the berg. The damaged vessel's SOS,
the responses of other ships, never reached him.

D. Nevertheless, the "Californian" was near enough for its
officers to see the "Titanic's" emergency rockets. They
were puzzled by them, but not enough to ask their
sleeping wireless operator to ask the "Titanic" about
them. The "Californian" did not learn of the catastrophe
until morning.

Conclusion

The warnings of icebergs ignored, safety precautions
slighted, communication with the nearest vessel broken, the
"Titanic" took to the bottom 1,500 persons who might have
been saved. Human error, as much as the iceberg, was the killer
that night in April, 1912.

The cause-and-effect relationship in this hypothetical speech is
rooted in past events. The collective error surrounding the collision
was the causal factor and the unnecessary loss of life the effect. The
striking of the iceberg in this instance was influential only so far as it
would have taken lives had the errors not been made. Had they not
been, there might have been no wreck; assuredly there would have
been a much greater saving of life.

The cause-and-effect pattern is by no means limited to past
events. Causal factors such as those of our "Titanic" illustration can
be used by a speaker to describe present circumstances about which
he may wish to warn his hearers. Human error, alas, did not disappear
with the "Titanic"; it still exists. A speaker might wish to remind us of
it. A series of plane crashes could be attributed to overcrowded skies,
a rash of auto accidents to haste and carelessness in manufacture. The
speaker would be relating effect to cause in a contemporary setting, or
possibly pointing to what might happen in greater degree if changes
are not made.

There is one special requirement for the cause-and-effect speech:

The factors cited must really be causal. It is not enough that certain things happened before something else. They must have brought it about or the speaker has no case. If the "Titanic" had sunk before there was any possibility of lowering boats, then the lack of boats could have cost no lives. It would not have been a causal factor. If the "Californian" could have been of no assistance in the rescue, then the break in wireless communication, though ironic, would not have been relevant nor causal of loss of life. In the instance of the plane crashes, no attribution to overcrowded skies would be valid if the planes went down because of internal explosions or weather conditions. And the car accidents could not be laid solely to faulty manufacture unless the mechanisms actually failed and all other factors were eliminated as possible causes.

I will mention this matter again in the section on persuasive speaking, but even in the informative speech the speaker has to be careful of the accuracy of his purported cause-and-effect relationships. Another logical pattern which we will explore in the chapter on persuasion is that of *problem–solution*. In this format the speaker poses a difficulty, offers potential solutions to it, narrows the field to the best one, and finally shows its superiority and workability.

THE RIGHT PATTERN

Other organizational patterns could be mentioned, but I have described the main ones. Certainly they are enough to show you the various paths you might take in organizing your speech and why it's important to think a little about the direction your talk might take.

Which is the right pattern for your next speech? Any one, two, or three of them. No rule states that you must follow only one or that a particular format is always most effective in a given situation.

Perhaps the best way of helping you decide which pattern to follow is to remind you of the key question of Chapter Two:

Why am I making this speech at this time to this audience?

You might be surprised how the asking of that question, followed by a little reflection, will lead you to the right approach to that speech coming up.

chapter 5

What's the Point?

You have witnessed it, I am sure. The speaker talks to his audience for ten minutes, perhaps longer—then, before his hearers have even realized he is finishing, he returns to his chair and the speech is over. The audience may be relieved or even delighted that it is, but blending with the signs of relief on the assembled faces is an expression of indifference which quashes all his oratorical efforts with a deadly implication. As one body the audience seems to be saying:

So—what else is new?

Obviously, you have no desire to find yourself in this fellow's position. Yet I must warn that there are two easy ways of getting there. One is by giving the audience little worth listening to before you reach your conclusion. The other is by bungling or entirely forgetting the conclusion itself.

As I hope to demonstrate in detail in the chapter that follows, your concluding remarks won't save you if the illustrations you used earlier weren't appropriate, if your comparisons were badly drawn, if the instances you cited in support of your thesis weren't valid, if the testimony you quoted did not come from qualified experts, if the statistics you enumerated weren't relevant.

"Tell me something I'll remember the rest of my life."

But, assuming these things are in order, and assuming your delivery was effective, what in particular is required of your closing remarks to produce a successful speech?

The first thing that might come to mind is a *summary*, a brief restatement of the main ideas. With few exceptions, this is a valuable device, particularly in an instructional speech. Yet rarely is the summary enough. It reviews what has gone ahead, but it does not drive home your theme. Suppose the determined Patrick Henry had stopped before:

> I know not what course others may take; but as for me, give me liberty or give me death!

Suppose Mr. Lincoln had folded his notes before resolving that "government of the people, by the people, and for the people, shall not perish from the earth."

Dramatic examples? Certainly, but I can scarcely overemphasize the importance of the conclusion. Far, far too often it is not only neglected—it is totally absent. That is, unless you consider a shrug and a "Well, that's about all I can think of," sufficient conclusion. Surely a speaker who has been talking to an audience for five minutes or more—taking their valuable time, if you will—can at least put what he has been saying into a good closing sentence or paragraph. If he can't, he is faced with a troubling question: "Have I really said anything?"

If a speaker can't wrap the speech into a tight package a few words long, how can he expect his audience to do so? Or does he expect his hearers to go away from the lecture hall repeating to themselves his every remark so that they may sort out his meaning?

STATEMENT OF THESIS

Adlai Stevenson, extraordinary speaker that he was, knew better than to leave a speech up in the air. He ended an address to a 1965 session of the United Nations Economic and Social Council at Geneva in this fashion:

> We travel together, passengers on a little space ship, dependent on its vulnerable reserves of air and soil; all committed for our safety to its security and peace; preserved from annihilation only by the care, the work, and, I will say, the love we give our fragile craft. We cannot maintain it half fortunate, half miserable, half confident, half despairing, half slave—to the ancient enemies of man—half free in a liberation of resources undreamed of until this day. No craft, no crew can travel safely with such vast contradictions. On their resolution depends the survival of us all.[1]

This conclusion may seem a trifle long by classroom standards, but it ended a formal and necessarily lengthy speech. In proportion to the over-all presentation it was no lengthier than a ten- or twenty-second finish to a five-minute speech would be. As a rule of thumb, incidentally, you might wish to remember that a conclusion should consume at least 5 per cent of the total speech. That's fifteen seconds of a five-minute talk, thirty seconds of a speech lasting ten minutes.

[1] Adlai Stevenson, "Strengthening the International Developmental Institutions," *Department of State Bulletin*, Vol. LIII, No. 1361 (July 26, 1965), 151. Also in *Speeches in English*, ed. Bower and Lucile F. Aly (New York: Random House, Inc., 1968), pp. 285–301.

PREDICTION

Mr. Stevenson's closing, as you may have surmised, formed a poignant statement of his central thesis. Another speaker adept at pouring the whole of his remarks into a compact capsule at the close of his remarks was Sir Winston Churchill. In his famous address to the American Congress following our entry into World War II, he managed to combine his optimistic thesis with another popular device for the conclusion: a look to the future.

> It is not given us to peer into the mysteries of the future; still I avow my hope and faith, sure and inviolate, that in the days to come the British and American peoples will for their own safety and for the good of all, walk together side by side in majesty, in justice, and in peace.[2]

Splendid as it was, don't let the rhetoric of Stevenson and Churchill persuade you that their techniques are beyond your skill. You may not match the majestic prose of these masters of oratory but, like them, you can end a speech with an accurate and concise asser-tion of your thesis—even if it's only "Boating offers refreshing escape to the troubled mind." What is more, as Churchill recognized, no human has special or exclusive power to peer into the future's mys-teries. You are therefore as entitled as any man or woman to direct an audience's thoughts to things yet to be. On some occasion, a pep rally for instance, it might prove a fine way of ending a speech.

QUOTATIONS

There are several other proven methods of bringing your speech to an end. One is to use a quotation appropriate to your thesis and objective. It may, in fact, state your thesis for you:

> *Oh wad some power the giftie gie us*
> *To see oursels as others see us!*
> (Robert Burns,
> "To a Louse")

[2] "Address of the Right Honorable Winston Churchill, delivered before the Con-gress of the United States, on December 26, 1941," *Congressional Record* (Wash-ington, D.C.: Government Printing Office, 1941), p. 10117. Also in Aly, *Speeches in English*, pp. 230-38, and *New York Times*, December 27, 1941.

or:

If Winter comes, can Spring be far behind?
(Percy Bysshe Shelley,
"Ode to the West Wind")

Most speech-ending quotations are from speeches, books, or poems. Sometimes, however, an effective ending can be fashioned from a chance expression of the average man on the street or of someone in the family. An almost-forgotten Army song was turned by General Douglas MacArthur into a striking means of closing an address to Congress following his removal from duty in the Korean War:

> I am closing my 52 years of military service. When I joined the Army even before the turn of the century, it was the fulfillment of all my boyish hopes and dreams. The world has turned over many times since I took the oath on the plain at West Point, and the hopes and dreams have long since vanished. But I still remember the refrain of one of the most popular barrack ballads of that day which proclaimed most proudly that—
> "Old soldiers never die; they just fade away."
> And like the old soldier of that ballad, I now close my military career and just fade away—an old soldier who tried to do his duty as God gave him the light to see that duty.
> Good-by.[3]

Fade away? Not Douglas MacArthur, who used the old refrain to cap his defense of his action in Korea—"his duty as God gave him to see that duty." He did not go into retirement for several years, and made one more memorable speech before gaining his rest.

Another American leader who ably drew upon song lyrics for a famous closing was Martin Luther King, Jr. In the speech at the Washington monument in 1963, he began his conclusion with the words of one selection and ended it with those of another:

> [W]e will be free one day. This will be the day when all God's children will be able to sing with new meaning—"my country

---

[3] Douglas MacArthur, "Address of General of the Army Douglas MacArthur, delivered before the Congress of the United States on April 19, 1951," *Congressional Record* (Washington, D.C.: Government Printing Office, 1951), p. 4125. Also in Aly, *Speeches in English*, pp. 250–59.

'tis of thee; sweet land of liberty; of thee I sing; land where my fathers died, land of the pilgrim's pride; from every mountain side, let freedom ring"—and if America is to be a free nation, this must become true.

So let freedom ring. . . .

And when we allow freedom to ring, when we let it ring from every village and hamlet, from every state and city, we will be able to speed up that day when all God's children—black men and white men, Jews and Gentiles, Catholics and Protestants —will be able to join hands and to sing in the words of the old Negro spiritual, "Free at last, free at last; thank God Almighty, we are free at last." [4]

If you select a quotation as the means of ending your speech, make sure that it is appropriate—to your thesis and to the occasion. Need we mention the possible repercussions of quoting the elder Hatfield to a meeting of the McCoys, or Henry Ford to a meeting of Chrysler executives? And be certain you have the quotation exact. Your conclusion isn't helped any if your audience is busy mentally correcting your wording. Even if you think you know the lines perfectly, a minute's checking might be worthwhile.

How often, for instance, have you heard someone say, "Money is the root of all evil"? Probably many times. Yet it would be dangerous, and possibly misleading, to end (or build) an argument on that quotation. Somebody is sure to retort that the passage in I Timothy (6:10) begins, "For the *love* of money is the root of all evil. . . ." Diogenes and Juvenal also used words meaning "love of money" in similar passages.

In speeches about personal rights we frequently hear another half-quotation. Former Supreme Court Justice Oliver Wendell Holmes is supposed to have said:

> Freedom of speech does not protect someone who shouts "Fire!" in a theatre.

Holmes' actual statement was much narrower:

> The most stringent protection of free speech would not

[4] Martin Luther King, Jr., "I Have a Dream," in Matson, *Voices in Crisis*, pp. 160-61.

protect a man in *falsely* shouting fire in a theatre and *causing a panic*. [Italics added.] [5]

The time spent in checking "familiar" quotations brings good return if effective conclusion is your goal. It is a shame to undo your own argument by borrowing words that were never said.

In any event, write the quotation down. It's horribly embarrassing to forget what you're quoting, particularly if you say something about "the immortal words" of So-and-so. Not long ago on national television a veteran actor forgot the immortal words with which he was closing a show and neither his co-host nor anyone within whispering range could remember them. The program left the air with the poor chap still fumbling for the rest of that line that supposedly meant so much to him. Immortal words have a way of hiding in the corner at times.

ILLUSTRATIONS

Just as you can use the illustrative story in your introduction to set up the thesis, you can use one in your conclusion to reinforce it. Once again, it must flow naturally from your speech, relate to the subject at hand, and be appropriate to the occasion. If it meets these criteria, an illustrative story can be a most effective way of rounding off your remarks.

Not that it's infallible. Occasionally, and you might as well recognize it, the most carefully arranged illustrations do not come through to some listeners. I remember the pastor of a small church in Pennsylvania who unfolded the story of David and Goliath to the youngsters of his flock at a children's service. He told of the fear which the giant struck in the hearts of the Israelites, and how no champion of Saul's army had the courage to meet him. Then he told of the bravery of the young shepherd boy who said he would fight the terrifying Philistine.

Now came the description of the skepticism in Saul's camp about the chances of a young boy against a great warrior, the surprise when David, who was ceremoniously clad in fine armor for the battle, took it off, saying he would fight Goliath just as he was, with only a staff and sling to aid him. Finally, there was the narration of the memorable confrontation and David's victory.

[5] Oliver Wendell Holmes, Majority Opinion, *Schenck v. United States*, 1919.

At last it was time for the moral. And the preacher, thinking he had shown that even the young can do great things if they have faith and courage, saw fit to ask his youthful hearers what they had learned from the story. Neither he nor the older members of the congregation were prepared for the response of the little one seated in the third pew. Demonstrating clearly how the lessons of religion can be confused with the exhortations of Mommy, this lad announced his own moral for the tale of David and Goliath:

> If you're gonna get into a fight, be sure to take off your good clothes.

STATEMENT OF PERSONAL INTENTION

A conclusion often can be made more forceful if the speaker relates himself to it through some planned action or position. This, of course, was what Patrick Henry was doing when he said, "I know not what course others may take, but as for me. . . ."

Presidential candidates almost always end their acceptance speeches in this fashion. These were Senator Barry Goldwater's closing words at the Republican convention in 1964:

> I repeat, I accept your nomination with humbleness, with pride, and you and I are going to fight for the goodness of our land.[6]

With slight variation you could use these words to your club or fraternity or sorority after being elected into office, or to your athletic team after they've named you captain, or to any other group that has given you a position of trust.

Even when the years remaining to you are few, this device can remain effective. Douglas MacArthur, in that last memorable speech mentioned earlier, closed his farewell to the cadet corps at West Point, May 12, 1962, in this eloquent manner:

> The shadows are lengthening for me. The twilight is here. My days of old have vanished—tone and tints. They have gone glimmering through the dreams of things that were. Their

[6] Barry Goldwater, "I Accept Your Nomination," in Matson, *Voices in Crisis*, p. 126.

memory is one of wondrous beauty, watered by tears and coaxed and caressed by the smiles of yesterday. I listen then, but with thirsty ear, for the witching melody of faint bugles blowing reveille, of far dreams beating the long roll.

In my dreams I hear again the crash of guns, the rattle of musketry, the strange, mournful mutter of the battlefield. But in the evening of my memory I come back to West Point. Always there echoes and re-echoes: Duty, honor, country.

Today marks my final roll call with you. But I want you to know that when I cross the river, my last conscious thoughts will be of the corps, and the corps, and the corps.

I bid you farewell.[7]

General MacArthur, incidentally, combined the technique of personal intention with that of quotation. "The corps, and the corps, and the corps" are the final words of one of the Military Academy's traditional songs.

CHALLENGE

Many fine speeches have ended with a challenge to the listeners. You've seen hundreds of fictional ones in motion pictures and television, some a trifle florid:

All right, men. This is it. The time we've waited for, fought for, suffered for has come. When you get the signal to jump, hit the silk with a determination that says: "We're coming at you, down there. And when we're finished you'll be sorry you tangled with the good old U.S.A."

If you missed that inspirational message on the late show, you must have caught this one:

Remember Casimir Klauslocowiecz. He was the best half-back this college ever had. And in the hospital room that last day he said, "Coach, whenever things get tough, and it looks like we're not going to pull the game out, tell the guys to win this one for old Caz."

This is that time, fellas. The time to win one for old Caz.

---

[7] Douglas MacArthur, "Duty, Honor, Country," in Matson, *Voices in Crisis,* p. 25.

I want you to knock down the doors of the locker room and get out there and show 50,000 people that this team came to play.

I suppose that things like this have been so done to death in dramatized situations that it's possible to forget that this method of closing a speech is enormously effective when used correctly. Haven't you been in a situation where it was? If you want bold and forceful action, you have to issue a strong challenge to your team, to your platoon, to your organization, to your country.

Of all the challenges issued to a nation, was any more stirring or more significant than the one Winston Churchill spoke to the British people in 1940, when Hitler's forces were poised across the English Channel and Great Britain stood alone against them?

> What General Weygand called the Battle of France is over. The Battle of Britain is about to begin.
>
> . . . The whole fury and might of the enemy must very soon be turned upon us. Hitler knows he will have to break us in this island or lose the war.
>
> If we can stand up to him all Europe may be freed and the life of the world may move forward into broad sunlit uplands; but if we fail, the whole world, including the United States and all that we have known and cared for, will sink into the abyss of a new dark age made more sinister and perhaps more prolonged by the lights of a perverted science.
>
> Let us therefore brace ourselves to our duty and so bear ourselves that if the British Commonwealth and Empire last for a thousand years, men will still say "This was their finest hour." [8]

PHRASES TO AVOID

Perhaps of all the segments of a speech the conclusion suffers the most from trite or ill-chosen expressions. The "Well-that's-about-all-I-can-think-of" approach I have already mentioned. The inevitable silent reply to that is, "Thank heavens!"

But there are other departing phrases we could wonder about. How about this one?

And now, without further ado . . .

[8] Winston Churchill, "The Battle of Britain," *New York Times,* June 19, 1940.

This must be a line you've heard 300 times. It stands only a slight level above "That's about all I can think of," and means the speaker hasn't figured out any other way of ending his speech. "Ado," incidentally, means bustling excitement, turmoil, trouble, difficulty. Considering some speeches, it may not be such a bad phrase after all.

Another phrase we could question the advantage of is:

And now in concluding may I say . . .

Possibly this announcement could be reassuring to those who have heard the speaker drone endlessly on, but far too often it is a decoy that offers false hope. It generally means that the speaker knows he has exceeded his allotted time, yet doesn't know enough to sit down. He thinks he can ease the minds of his hearers by suggesting he is concluding.

There is another thing wrong with pointedly telling your audience you are finishing. Even if you're honest about it, you are giving the audience a cue to do other things: to stop listening and begin putting on their coats, to fold up the printed program and put it away, to get ready to dash toward the exit, to stop taking notes, to do anything else but what you intend them to do, that is, pay close attention to your closing remarks. "And now in concluding" might well be consigned to the graveyard of outworn endings.

One that is almost ready to join it is "Thank you." Is it really necessary to express your gratitude to your audience each and every time you leave the lectern? I don't mean to outlaw courtesy or to say that you never should thank an audience, but do reserve your thanks for unusual situations in which they may be particularly in order. The tone of your voice can let your audience know you are ending, and your manner and bearing can tell them you appreciate their time. The only real way to thank an audience, remember, is to give them a good speech.

AFTER THE TALK

Not all speaking situations end with your conclusion. You will often be called upon to answer questions. Some you will be able to answer, some you won't, and some you will have answered already in your speech. If the question suggests that the asker wasn't listening, refrain from telling him so. Give a brief answer and go on to someone else. If you don't know the full answer, honesty is your best path. Respond as well as you can, then stop. Audiences generally can tell when you're faking.

As a general rule, when a member of the audience asks a question, repeat it before giving the answer. There are three advantages to this: (1) you make sure that the rest of the audience hears it; (2) you make sure that you have heard it correctly; and (3) you give yourself a little time to organize your thoughts before responding.

Do not be worried or offended if the audience fires a lot of questions at you. It is a sign that your speech aroused their interest.

SUPPORTING MATERIAL

chapter 6

Words in Support

We have considered ways of narrowing a broad subject to one appropriate to your objective and audience, one that can be captured in a thesis sentence. We have also considered patterns of organization and basic techniques which will carry your ideas from introduction to conclusion. Now it is time to look at the means of upholding or enlarging upon those ideas, for rarely can a speech be successful without some kind of supporting material.

Essentially, the points you offer in a speech will stand or fall depending upon how well you make use of *fact*, of *opinion*, and of the various *rhetorical devices* available to you. I will explain each of these categories as they relate in general fashion to public speaking. The nature of the individual speech, of course, ordinarily determines the extent to which you call upon a particular kind of support. An entertainment speech might contain little in the way of facts, figures, or opinions, yet might be loaded with rhetorical devices such as anecdotes, humorous definitions, and colorful descriptions. An explanatory talk, on the other hand, might stress figures and facts, include some opinion, and not contain a single story. A persuasive speech quite likely will draw upon all the means of support, in ways that will be considered in a later section of the book. For the moment, though, let's examine the several means of support as they should be treated in even the simplest of speech settings.

FACTUAL SUPPORT

At first thought the category of factual support seems simple enough. In presenting his argument or instruction, the speaker calls upon the facts which show how he reached the truth of the matter and which buttress his position. And really that's the way it is—if we agree that man can reason his way to truth. This question is one that could be argued for the rest of this volume and twenty more, without producing an answer that would satisfy everyone. It's a question so old that Aristotle had something to say about it 2,300 years ago. In addition to the natural reasons for a philosopher to wonder about truth, Aristotle had before him the arguments of the Skeptics, who said that man could know nothing for certain, that any proposition was as likely to be false as to be true. Aristotle made short work of these fellows in his *Metaphysics*. If their argument was correct, he countered, then their insistence that nothing was certain could not itself be verified. Further, if nothing could be known to be true, why, Aristotle wondered, did men not stroll off the edges of cliffs or into wells instead of avoiding such disasters?

Unless we plan to band with the Skeptics, we must admit that there are things that can be called facts and that they can be woven together by logical reasoning to produce truths. We may have special requirements for accepting or rejecting material put forth as factual, as in a court of law, but we can agree that some things exist, or have occurred, which are substantial enough to be called facts, and that we build our lives as well as our speeches upon them. We see each night the fact that is the moon. We reason to the greater fact (or truth) that it is a barren globe, a satellite of our earth. We at last visit that satellite and confirm the long-held reasoning.

Some people, of course, hold rigid standards as to what they will accept as fact. They proclaim that they will believe only what they see (or can duplicate, as in a scientific experiment). Such individuals rarely recognize that in the course of life they have unconsciously accepted thousands of facts—for instance, that the four-legged, friendly creature which wags its tail is a dog. More important, they seldom realize that what they have "seen" may or may not have occurred as they "saw" it or remember it. They may have observed the happening too carelessly, or with too much prejudice, to see it as it was. Staged incidents in psychology classes have vividly demonstrated the many different ways a brief action can be interpreted by its witnesses. At times, sound reasoning based upon accurate reports can be more meaningful than being there.

Facts Based upon Personal Observation

When you use a fact based upon your own observation—and it is perfectly acceptable in a speech to do so—be sure that you test it as carefully as you would an assertion by another speaker. Take care that memory or emotion has not colored your interpretation of that confrontation between police and demonstrators. Acknowledge at least the possibility of observational error. Aside from this due caution, however, don't hold back from using an appropriate bit of personal reporting that will enhance your presentation.

As with any fact, however, don't stretch things too far. If you have counted heads and found that, in addition to yourself, your happy household contains one mother, one father, three sisters, four brothers, one dog, one cat, and four goldfish, don't expect this kernel of data to help you much with the thesis, "All large families have great fun," or in an argument that a second bathroom is only a luxury. A good fact will not undergird a proposition that goes farther than the evidence allows, nor one that is primarily a matter of opinion and personal preference.

Factual Data Provided by External Sources

Although in our daily lives we encounter a great number of incidents which provide us with factual information, we derive much of our *factual data from others.* We certainly weren't there, yet we know that Columbus sailed for America in 1492, that George Washington was our first President, that Lincoln was assassinated by John Wilkes Booth, that a sneak attack precipitated our entrance into World War II, and so on. Indeed, we formally joined the global conflict in 1941 following an awesome reporting of facts by our Chief Executive in his war message to Congress. From its first sentence, President Roosevelt's address was an example of factual argument:

Yesterday, December 7, 1941—a date that will live in infamy—the United States of America was suddenly and deliberately attacked by naval and air forces of the Empire of Japan.

The succeeding sentences described the negotiations with Japan going on in Washington at the time of the air and naval strikes. Then Mr. Roosevelt revealed how factual material can be molded into the reasoning processes:

It will be recorded that the distance of Hawaii from Japan makes it obvious that the attack was deliberately planned many days or even weeks ago. During the intervening time the Japanese government has deliberately sought to deceive the United States by false statements and expressions of hope for continued peace.

A paragraph on American losses was followed by a devastating series of factual statements virtually mandating a war declaration:

Yesterday the Japanese government also launched an attack against Malaya. Last night Japanese forces attacked Hong Kong. Last night Japanese forces attacked Guam. Last night Japanese forces attacked the Philippine Islands. Last night the Japanese attacked Wake Island. This morning the Japanese attacked Midway Island.

Now a summary of the evidence:

Japan has, therefore, undertaken a surprise offensive extending throughout the Pacific area. The facts of yesterday speak for themselves.

And, after some words designed to inspire and give confidence to the American people, came the request for a declaration of war that President Roosevelt believed the facts wholly justified:

I ask that the Congress declare that since the unprovoked and dastardly attack by Japan on Sunday, December seventh, a state of war has existed between the United States and the Japanese Empire.[1]

[1] Franklin Delano Roosevelt, "Address to the Congress, December 8, 1941," *Congressional Record* (Washington, D.C.: Government Printing Office, 1941), pp. 9504-5.

The declaration President Roosevelt requested followed almost immediately.

Testing Facts. While the actuality of the 1941 attacks was not questioned (there being overwhelming documentation and verification by all military and civilian channels), matters of evidence are rarely so clear-cut. Reports by others, whatever their station in life, must bear scrutiny if they are offered as bases for action or judgment. Without becoming latter-day Skeptics, we have to make sure the facts presented by others are facts before we act upon them or attach them to our own speeches or writings.

Did, for instance, that person who saw a flying saucer have any evidence to show that it was a spaceship he saw, and not an optical illusion created by light reflection, or possibly a weather balloon? If he claims he has evidence, what kind is it? Some knickknacks he could have fabricated himself? A rambling story of being taken for a spin by the little green men who communicated with him by thought transference? Are these things evidence?

Other questions might be asked. Is there anything that could cause the witness to the saucer episode (or any other incident) to see the action somewhat differently than it really was? Could he have reason to distort the truth—to lie, if you prefer? Remember we often see what we wish to see, and some people aren't too careful about the truth, in conversation or in print. Persons who have axes to grind, who need attention, who have excess loyalty to particular groups are not the most trustworthy reporters.

When you come across seemingly factual material you might like to use in a speech, ask yourself if the originator of that material has reason to be biased. Would you, for example, expect to find a student sit-in reported in the same way in a conservative journal as you would in a college newspaper? Is either publication likely to be as accurate about that kind of incident as it would be about a less volatile subject? It is well, then, to consider the source of the information when examining apparently factual matter. This is especially true for subjects in controversy. Always pause to ask yourself if the material at hand is likely to be valid. Often it will be, yet not everything that finds its way into print is above suspicion. You must evaluate each potential piece of support to the degree you would wish others to do so.

If the source of a piece of factual information appears to be reliable but you still are not satisfied of the material's validity, you can examine it internally to good end. First of all you can decide if there is reasonable *probability* that the fact at hand is true. You cannot, of course, convert probability into either truth or falsehood. Some quite improbable things, such as camels and kangaroos, do exist. But if the fact seems unlikely on the surface, you have all the more reason to test it further. Do the several parts of a report hold together well? Is it consistent within itself, in other words? A report of a heavy battle which contains a paragraph indicating light casualties would seem on the face of things to have some inconsistency.

The *number of observers*, or reporters, of an occurrence may also be meaningful in questionable items. How many people witnessed and commented upon the alleged happening? One observer cannot build a good case for the existence of the Abominable Snowman.

You might also ask yourself if the *whole story* seems to have been told in the account you have before you. A popular weekly magazine is notorious for its distortions of fact through the deliberate omission of key points. Be wary of the three dots . . . which indicate that part of a quotation has been left out. Be alert for a string of details all on one side of an issue. Rarely are things either all black or all white. Be suspicious also of clever phrases or statements that can have two meanings. In sum, look carefully at the "fact" and let your natural good sense help you evaluate it.

Testing Statistics. The same caution holds for statistics, a favorite device of many speakers. There are statistical data which represent fact, and which, when used with care and fairness, can advance a case. But recognize the difference between the counted and the estimated. If you are talking about the amount of food the world will need in 2000 A.D., it is obvious that you are presenting an estimate. It is not always realized that it is an estimate based upon an estimate. No one knows for sure how many people there will be in 2000 A.D., so it is something of a guess how much food they will need. Future population predictions are based heavily upon the populations of large countries, notably China and India—lands whose populations today can only be roughly approximated. Beware, then, of anchoring an argument on birth control or undersea farming on a guess. At least, tell the audience that it is a guess.

Do not, we should add, let the appearance of a statistic in a newsmagazine fool you into accepting it as gospel. To give an impression of veracity, the best-known weeklies pack articles with interesting data—the number of acres devoted to raising peas in Madagascar, the percentage of decline in unemployment in Tibet, the number of suits in a dictator's closet, the number of tanks in his army. It is little known that the writers of these articles prepare them with blank spaces where the statistics will go. Young editorial assistants called "checkers" fill in the blanks. If they can obtain official figures, they or their superiors have the choice of using them or, if they seem exaggerated, adjusting them to proper size. If no figures are available, they can estimate. After all, who knows how many peas are grown in Madagascar?

When a newsmagazine is the source of a statistic you would like to use, first ask yourself: "Could anyone really have authenticated this figure?" A "no" answer means that if you use it, the audience should be advised of both its source and its hypothetical nature. A "yes" answer means that the statistic may be accurate but that a look at another source might be worthwhile. Almanacs, encyclopedias, dictionaries, and bound reference works tend to be more reliable than newsmagazines. Newspapers may or may not be reliable, in part depending on whether there was time to check the material before going to press.

One more suggestion here: If you decide to use a news item or a statistic, give your audience reasonable opportunity to evaluate it by naming your source:

> According to an account in *TIME* . . .
>
> In the *New York Times* Tom Wicker reported . . .
>
> Statistics provided by the Tobacco Research Council indicate that . . .
>
> My Great-aunt Daphne says that on the day he should have been voting for Prohibition she saw Senator Birdbath in a restaurant with Eliza Cumquat.

OPINION

Testimonial Support

Not every speech topic can be, or need be, supported by cold facts. Sometimes matters are beyond material proof, or at least years away from it. And yet often action must be taken when the absolute evidence is too thin for any certainty. At times the best that can be hoped for is a correct decision based upon probability. In situations such as these, testimonial support, normally in the form of an expressed opinion, can be of service.

Testimony can be to fact, of course:

> The Secretary of Health, Education, and Welfare has announced that 900,000 Americans are currently on regional welfare rolls.

Here the prestige of the Secretary of Health, Education, and Welfare's office adds stature to the statistic, assuming his reputation is unsullied by scandal.

But what of those times when even a Cabinet secretary does not have documented evidence at his fingertips? Can his statements still aid you? Of course they can—if he is speaking or writing in an area in which he is an authority. Cabinet secretaries are expected to have knowledge and experience in their areas of specialization. So are professors, and scientists, and football coaches. They may not always be right, but they are specialists. When commenting on their fields of knowledge they usually receive respect.

Do not expect, however, that the insertion of a statement by a labor-management expert will help you much in a lecture on raising petunias. Unless a man is noted as much for his hobby as for his vocation, his testimony won't help much outside his area of proficiency. At your own risk, therefore, use the opinion of a baseball manager in a talk on blending colors in a drawing room. It is to your advantage, though, to use his theory on when to bunt with men on base if you are talking about baseball.

These examples may seem farfetched, yet they aren't nearly as extreme or as dangerous as many instances in real life. All too often the words of an eminent man of science are used to support arguments in which his opinion is no more meaningful or valid than that of the next man. When selecting a statement of another individual to back up a proposition, reflect upon his qualifications as an expert. If he is commenting out of his field, think twice about using his opinion.

In some situations, incidentally, the expert may be you. Why not, if you have become adept at a particular skill or hobby, tell the audience what techniques have worked well for you? As long as you let your listeners know that your viewpoint is based upon some amount of experience, you are employing an honest and valuable technique. Indeed, it is reassuring to hear that a speaker is using the ideas he is talking about. You'll find this especially true in speeches of demonstration. Add *personal testimony* whenever it is appropriate.

Public Opinion

Thus far we have mentioned only individual opinion, expert or personal. Another kind of opinion that a speaker must recognize and perhaps call upon is the familiar public opinion. It can be a potent force for or against a thesis, strong enough at times to outweigh factual argument. Several years ago the Ford Motor Company introduced an automobile that was sound mechanically and contained features of design which would be used in other cars later on. But the public did not take to the Edsel, apparently because its features and appearance were not what the people wanted in the period when large, elaborate cars were momentarily in a decline and the compact car was becoming popular. Once the Edsel had fallen into disdain, no factual argument about its mechanical excellence could make the car a good buy. Opinion was more important than fact.

Ironically, the car manufacturer had surveyed the tastes of the buying public before launching the new vehicle. But there was too long a period between idea and execution: By the time the first cars had rolled off the assembly line, the fickle car-buying public had other ideas about the ideal automobile. The Edsel was doomed, as the Packard had been a short time earlier, and as other seemingly established cars had been which were caught for various reasons in the spokes of transition: the Nash, the Studebaker, the DeSoto. It must have been small comfort to the Edsel's designers to see the car of another manufacturer attain great success with the supposedly unacceptable vertical grille while used Edsels became overpriced collector's items.

I don't mean to imply that public opinion changes as rapidly in all matters as it does in automobile preferences. Nonetheless, it is never constant and should not be thought of as such. The only way to measure it, short of an election, is through carefully designed opinion polls of representative samples of the populace, conducted with some regularity. If the poll is not well designed, the results can be disastrous. On some issues, moreover, many people will not answer honestly no matter how careful the questioning. The so-called "white backlash" is almost impossible to measure accurately, for example.

Use the results of public-opinion surveys if you wish, but use them carefully. They must be up-to-date. They must be from reputable, unprejudiced sources. They must be presented only as what they are:

samplings of opinion which are probable, but not certain, representations of a group's sentiments. If you yourself are the poll taker—as you might be in preparation for a speech in which student or organizational opinion is important—select your respondents with a view to balance. If an issue crosses lines of age, sex, economic status, and religion, don't survey only girls, or car owners, or Presbyterians. The percentage breakdown of your sample group should be close to that of the group as a whole. The larger your sample, of course, the more impressive your homemade survey can be. Do not expect to get far with a statement like this:

> Surely Reginald is the most qualified candidate for student body president; all his fraternity brothers, as well as his mother, think so.

Quotations

Although we have emphasized using others' words when they reflect fact or expert knowledge, quotations can enrich a presentation if they are simply well-phrased statements on life in general. Especially is this true if the originators of the statements are people of renown. To use the words of another properly is to call him to your side as you present your speech. For example:

> As Voltaire put it, "Whoever serves his country well has no need of ancestors."

or

> In the words of Mark Twain, "One of the most striking differences between a cat and a lie is that a cat has only nine lives."

Where do you find quotations that can help you add color and impact to a speech? Well, naturally, you can use things that you have heard people say, even those in your own family. The trouble is that you will not run across too many original gems of discourse in a lifetime. And if you hear someone quoting another, you have to hope that he got the statement right and that you remember it correctly. A safer way of finding the special words you need lies in consulting the reference books of quotations.

The most famous compilation of quotations is John Bartlett's *Familiar Quotations*. The first edition of this venerable reference book appeared in 1855. Since that time there have been many revisions to keep the selections close to the attitudes of the time. The second major reference work of this type was *The Home Book of Quotations*, edited by Burton Stevenson in 1934 and, like Bartlett's book, revised many times since. A little later came *The Oxford Dictionary of Quotations* (first edition in 1941), H. L. Mencken's *A New Dictionary of Quotations* (1942), and *FPA's Book of Quotations* (1952). The year 1960 brought *The Great Quotations*, compiled by George Seldes, who believed that the statements collected in the other reference works were too frequently on the safe or sentimental side. Bergen Evans' *Dictionary of Quotations* was published in 1968.

All these dictionaries of quotations are useful, despite their variations in approach. Your library probably contains some edition of at least one of them, and you may wish to acquire a low-priced version for home use. The books are arranged by author, with cross-reference indexing to subjects (e.g., Justice, Love), or they are arranged by subject with cross-references to authors. Both patterns have advantages, as you will recognize when you begin using the books.

As in other uses of fact or opinion, when drawing upon a philosophical or humorous quotation, be sure to name the source—at least the author and, when important, the book or speech from which the words were taken. It is not necessary, though, to become a living footnote. Blend the citation into your remarks in a natural manner. Just as you don't wish the listener to wonder where those choice words came from, you don't wish to smother him in publication data.

RHETORICAL DEVICES

We have used this designation to cover the several ways a speaker can support his ideas through verbal means: *definition, description, rhetorical comparison, illustration, repetition,* and *restatement.* These may be arbitrary categories, but as I explain them you should be able to see what is meant by each one.

Definition

Sometimes the most important single thing you can do in a speech is to tell the audience exactly what you are talking about, over-

"*I am an over-thirty. Hath not an over-thirty eyes? Hath not an over-thirty hands, organs, dimensions, senses, affections, passions? If you prick us, do we not bleed? If you tickle us, do we not laugh? If you poison us, do we not die? And if you wrong us, should we not revenge?*"

all or in a particular section of the talk. If you present an argument relating to communism, make sure that those listening know whether you are talking about a political theory or the particular form of government practiced in Soviet Russia. It can be disastrous to plod through a speech when you have one idea of what you are talking about and the audience another. Examine your speech for key terms, and if there is any possibility of misunderstanding, clarify them. If you can add a specific example to the definition, so much the better.

Though the dictionary will be the best place to find a formal definition, your general reading, a book of quotations, or your own ingenuity might bring you a crisp statement that could be of service in those instances when emphasis or color is needed. Surely Winston Churchill was enlarging upon Webster when he offered:

> A fanatic is one who can't change his mind and won't change the subject.

Description

Involving more words, normally, than a definition, description is the speaker's verbal equivalent to drawing a picture. It should not be florid, any more than a good drawing or painting should. A description should be long enough to do the job and no longer, should not be loaded with adjectives, and should have both purpose and plan. Don't expect an audience to sit contentedly through a display of supposed elegance in phrasemaking if the description seems to have no reason for being or shows no care in organization.

While frequently we think of description in terms of physical entities—towns, countryside, people—it may be significant to describe a condition. Here is how Frederick Douglass, himself born in slavery, portrayed the legal status of the slave for the citizens of Rochester, New York, on December 1, 1850:

> The law gives the master absolute power over the slave. He may work him, flog him, hire him out, sell him, and in certain circumstances, *kill* him, with perfect impunity. . . . His name . . . is impiously inserted in a *master's ledger*, with horses, sheep, and swine. In law, the slave has no wife, no children, no country, and no home. He can own nothing, possess nothing, acquire nothing, but what must belong to another. To eat the fruit of his own toil, to clothe his person with the work of his own hands, is considered stealing. He toils that another may reap the fruit; he is industrious that another may live in idleness; he eats unbolted meal, that another may eat the bread of fine flour; he labors in chains at home, under a burning sun and biting lash, that another may ride in ease and splendor abroad; he lives in ignorance, that another may be educated; he is abused that another may be exalted; he rests his toil worn limbs on the cold, damp ground, that another may repose on the softest pillow; he is clad in coarse and tattered raiment, that another may be arrayed in purple and fine linen; he is sheltered only

by the wretched hovel, that a master may dwell in a magnificent
mansion; and to this condition he is bound down as by an arm
of iron.[2]

Rhetorical Comparison

As you read Frederick Douglass' description of the legal status
of the slave, you must have recognized that toward the latter part he
was enlarging his description by contrasting in vivid language the life
of slave and master. Description often becomes more graphic when
one thing is put beside another—something that it is like or something
that it is unlike. This is especially true when the thing being described
is beyond concrete measurement, when expressive language can give
it a clarity it might not derive from ordinary definition or description.
At such times the speaker, striving to clarify the abstract, employs
rhetorical rather than measurable units of expressing sameness or
otherness. Notice how Adlai Stevenson contrasted nonphysical concepts to extend and enrich the dictionary definition of patriotism in a
speech before the American Legion in Madison Square Garden, August
27, 1952:

> Patriotism is not the fear of something; it is the love of
> something. . . . Patriotism with us is not hatred of Russia; it
> is love of this republic; it is love of the ideal of liberty of man
> and of mind in which this country was born and to which it is
> dedicated.

Mark Twain used figurative contrast to show the importance of
careful word selection:

> The difference between the right word and the almost
> right word is the difference between lightning and the lightning
> bug.

Difference can be expressed effectively with numbers too. Suppose instead of the flat statistic:

> Thirty million people saw *Hamlet* on television last night.

[2] Frederick Douglass, *Lectures on American Slavery* (Buffalo: Reese & Company's
Power Press, 1851), as reprinted in Crosscup, *Classic Speeches,* pp. 185-86.

the speaker would say:

> To have reached as many people as saw *Hamlet* on television last night, a theatre company would have had to give 30,000 live performances in a theatre seating 1,000 persons. At the usual rate of nine performances a week, this would require, in contrast with television's one evening, slightly more than 64 years.

Statistics invariably are more understandable if they are put into meaningful terms, even if those terms are purely figurative, as in the above example. No one would really expect a theatre company to toil away at *Hamlet* for almost two-thirds of a century.

If sameness, not otherness, is what you wish to emphasize in your presentation, several choices are open to you. You may not know them by their technical names, but undoubtedly have used them. The *simile* is one such device. For instance:

> A tie game is like a kiss from your sister.

Similes normally contain the bridging words "as" or "like." Without the word bridge, simile becomes the more direct *metaphor*. *Peanuts* fans are familiar with metaphors, as in:

> Happiness is a warm puppy.

Both simile and metaphor are helpful in describing abstract ideas that seem beyond conventional definition. They also help when the dictionary statement seems too colorless for your purpose. As you listen to speeches, see how often these devices are used, then give a little thought to trying some of your own. Just be careful of the *mixed metaphor*, which is like mixing apples and oranges:

> It was like swimming through an avalanche of arrows.

A form of comparison extended beyond the length of simile or metaphor is *analogy*. While there are many variations of interpretation, an analogy is simply a comparison which assumes that if two (or more) things are alike in some ways they also will be alike in others.

If the details are real and the things compared are from the same general class—two football teams, for instance—the analogy is *literal*. If the things compared are of different classes—married life and an ocean crossing—the analogy is *figurative*.

The literal analogy, however, is no more likely to be valid than is the figurative one. In fact, it may be less so. Two real-life situations rarely are alike in all significant ways, thus many *false analogies* are drawn, accidently or deliberately. It is one thing to compare the operations of the heart with those of a pump. It is quite another to develop an analogy using the United States of today and the United States of President Washington's administration. The class is the same, but not the particulars, such as population density, principal source of income, foreign trade, industrial development, and so on. A literal analogy involving eras two centuries apart must be carefully drawn. Regrettably, politicians who love to hark back to the good old days are not very careful most of the time.

Undoubtedly you will use analogy in your speeches. As you do, remember that an analogy is never proof, just a means of comparison. A sound argument may contain an analogy, but the analogy remains an illustration. When you are comparing things of the same class in a literal analogy, examine the particulars carefully to make certain the situations are parallel. If they are not, discard the analogy—and take a good look at the case you are trying to make. If the case won't stand without the poor analogy, it is either invalid or very much in need of support of another kind. Possibly it is just a reasonable hypothesis, derived from, but not proved by, the analogy. That's all right as long as you don't try to make more of it.

When your analogy is figurative, your task is to see both that it is appropriate to the idea you wish to bring out and that it is well constructed. The suggestions in the next part of this chapter should help you put it together properly. An example might be of value also. Here is an analogy that the famed lawyer, Clarence Darrow, employed to support his theory that people, if given room and opportunity, do not lead criminal lives. Darrow's audience? The inmates of the Cook County jail. After talking of the good lives led by the convict settlers of Australia and parts of the South, Darrow said:

> Some of you people have lived in the country. It's prettier than it is here. And if you have ever lived on a farm you understand that if you put a lot of cattle in a field, when the pasture

is short they will jump over the fence; but put them in a good field where there is plenty of pasture, and they will be law-abiding cattle to the end of time. The human animal is just like the rest of the animals, only a little more so. The same thing that governs in the one governs in the other.[3]

Now that you have read Mr. Darrow's analogy, put it to a test. Is it appropriate to the point he wished to illustrate? In terms of the purpose of the illustration, are men and cows analogous? Does the analogy make his argument more concrete? Do you think the analogy is effective, whether or not it is valid? If it has a weak point, what is it?

Sorry, I won't provide any answers. I want you to think this one through.

The Illustration

A key device in rhetorical art, the illustration is a way of present-ing an example in narrative form. If the narrative is brief, perhaps only a line or two, the example is usually called an *instance*. There are, in the instance, the basic elements of a fact—names, numbers, places—but no development of details. Often a series of instances is used in the same speech. Notice what John F. Kennedy did in two paragraphs of a televised prenomination speech in Charleston, West Virginia, May 3, 1960:

> If there is one quality which I think this state can be justly proud of, it is the quality of courage.
>
> —More men from West Virginia lost their lives in the Korean War than from any state in the Union of its size.
> —More West Virginians served in World War II than for any state its size.
> —I was in Hinton this morning, which is the home of the navigator who flew with my brother before he was killed.
>
> This is a state which has sent men to die in every section of the world. And also here in the state of West Virginia you

[3] Clarence Darrow, "Address to Prisoners in Cook County Jail" (Chicago: Charles H. Kerr and Co., 1913), as reprinted in *The Speaker's Resource Book*, ed. Carroll C. Arnold, Douglas Ehninger, and John C. Gerber (Chicago: Scott, Foresman and Company, 1966), p. 145.

have the courage to work in the basic industry of this state—
coal mining.
  —Eight West Virginians die in the coal mines of this state
    every month.
These people are tough and hard; they've lived in the mountains;
  —there are probably more descendants of American revo-
    lutionary soldiers here in West Virginia than in any state
    of the country.[4]

For obvious reasons the *longer illustration,* or a story, is harder to construct than the instance. Yet it may be the most valuable support device available to a speaker. People generally enjoy hearing stories, and most of the time they learn or understand more from them than they do from formal reasoning. It is both interesting and meaningful that the two most famous users of the illustrative story are Jesus of Nazareth and Abraham Lincoln. Both relied upon stories to explain complexities to the common people, but both recognized that the device would work with any stratum of society. That an intellectual such as Adlai Stevenson employed the narrative frequently is further testimony to its universal value.

Now, there are many kinds of stories: fables, parables, anecdotes, historical incidents, and so on. Some authorities consider them categories separate from the illustration. For our purposes I am keeping them together to avoid getting lost in terminology. If your story is good—and illustrates what it is supposed to—it doesn't really matter what you call it. Rarely, in fact, do speakers label their stories. That doesn't mean, though, that they are unaware of the several kinds available to them or of their obligation not to deceive an audience by passing off a piece of imagination as history. Perhaps I can set up some general rules for storytelling that might help you whatever form you select:

1. *Be sure the story has a point.* A talk is no place for a shaggy dog tale. You need not think of the point as being something as somber as a moral, but any story inserted as a means of support should have a reason for being. State the point at the beginning or the end, according to what is appropriate. Or don't state it at all, if it can be

---

[4] John F. Kennedy, "West Virginia Debate, May 3, 1960," transcribed by the *Charleston Gazette,* May 5, 1960, and quoted with amendment in *Speeches for Illustration and Example,* ed. Goodwin F. Berquist, Jr. (Chicago: Scott, Foresman and Company, 1965), p. 160.

made by implication. Just don't waste people's time with something that doesn't advance the speech.

2. *As you prepare the story, set down the parts in brief form.* This will help you organize, and should reveal the main phases. Elements that are not essential can be eliminated before they reach the audience's ears. Select only the parts you need to give color to the story and to make the point.

3. *Arrange the parts so that they build toward a climax.* It need not be as dramatic as that of an Alfred Hitchcock movie, yet it should have more impact than any old sentence along the line. Stories, like speeches, should have introductions, bodies, and conclusions. In a humorous story the climax will normally fall in the last line, in a serious story somewhere in or near the last paragraph. Try to set it up by letting the preceding sections lead in its direction. If the climax involves a bit of a trick, don't spoil it by telegraphing the secret in advance. I remember one student's use of a story about a mysterious stranger who wandered into his house one evening and sat down in the middle of the living room. The student spoiled the suspense, though, by telling us too soon that the visitor was just a harmless drunk. After that, the five minutes of unusual doings the student recounted had no mystery, and the story lost its impact. His point, whatever it was, was lost. Another student had this kind of ruinous opening line:

> I'm going to tell you about the time we were arrested while driving through the desert, but it was all a mistake because they thought we were some other people.

What fun was there for the audience after that?

4. *As you tell the story, take the audience along.* Let them see the events as they unfold—just as if they were witnesses. By description let them see or hear what is important in following or appreciating the story. Without referring to such things as the rosy-fingered dawn, give them the necessary atmosphere for getting into the narrative. Adjectives are important, of course, but can be overdone. You can do as well with strong, well-selected verbs and some pieces of dialogue. Beginning speakers often overlook the usefulness of a bit of conversation in recreating a real incident or dramatizing a fictional one. Detail can be important, too. Little things go far in creating an over-all impression. Concise descriptions of several objects may do more for a

story than an extensive description of one. Try to picture each phase of the story in your mind, then select those elements of it that you would wish to hear if you were the listener.

An *anecdote*, naturally, does not require as much elaboration or detail as a narrative of some scope. But observe what Adlai Stevenson was able to put into a few lines—while making an amusing commentary on the small-town view of world fame:

> I had been away from my home town of Bloomington a number of years and was asked to return to give a speech. I had not expected a brass band, but I was a little surprised to find no welcoming committee. So I picked up my bag and as I passed Abe (an old baggageman who had known me since I was a boy), he raised his head and said, "Hello, Ad . . . been away?" [5]

5. *In telling a longer story, watch your transitions.* A personal experience can become most tedious if it is tied together by a string of "And then we's." Keep on the lookout for words such as "so," "then," "next," "and so," "well," and others of that kind. Use them sparingly, and don't think that every paragraph must begin with one of them—followed by a smack of the lips or a deep breath. If you sin heavily in this direction, you may have to write your transitional sentences on your speaking notes. A strong temptation to use "then we" may mean that you have not organized your story very well or selected its phases with a view to building toward a climax. All segments should not be of such equal importance and design that they can begin with the same little words.

6. *Avoid tense-hopping.* By that I mean: Select one verb tense, normally the past, and stay with it. People telling stories, particularly if they are personal experiences, tend to switch from the past tense to the present and then back again. They say things like this:

> We *started* for town at about eight o'clock and *got* there a half hour later. We *parked* outside the drug store and *went* in. Near the door we *see* this guy with a duck in his arms. As soon as he *sees* us he *heads* for the side exit. The druggist *goes* after him and we *followed* them on the dead run. . . .

[5] *The Wit and Wisdom of Adlai Stevenson*, comps. Edward Hanna, Henry Hicks, and Ted Koppel (New York: Hawthorn Books, Inc., 1965), pp. 90, 92.

To slip into tense-hopping is dangerously easy, because we hear it or do it so often in ordinary conversation. But while it's scarcely noticed in a cafeteria get-together, it takes the polish off the narrative in a speech. Treat tense-hopping as you would eating peas with a knife; it can be done, but it spoils the effect.

7. *Keep your mood appropriate to the story.* Don't look sternly at the audience throughout a lighthearted account of your first date. On the other hand, don't be afraid to be serious if that is what the occasion demands. One student speaker, accustomed only to speaking to his classmates in carefree manner, grew self-conscious when telling them of a swimming disaster he witnessed. He actually said something like this:

> This one kid couldn't swim. [Quick smile.] I saw him go down for the second time, and then the third. [Heh-heh.] And he didn't come up. [Hah-hah-hah-hah.]

Treat adults, classmates included, as adults. They would not laugh at a drowning and would not think you square for presenting the matter in straightforward fashion. This point is worth remembering.

Whether your story is incident or fable, anecdote or parable, put care into its preparation and enthusiasm into its delivery. A story well told will carry you far. It might reach your listener more effectively and stay with him longer than any other part of your speech.

Repetition and Restatement

Whatever the rhetorical device or fact or quotation you use, it can at times be strengthened by *repetition*. Surely you remember the increasing irony in Marc Anthony's:

> *Yet Brutus says he was ambitious;*
> *And Brutus is an honorable man.*

Shakespeare, trained in classical rhetoric, knew the value of repetition for impact. So did President Kennedy that day in West Berlin:

> There are many people in the world who really don't understand, or say they don't, what is the great issue between the free world and the Communist world.
> —Let them come to Berlin.

There are some who say that communism is the wave of the future.

—Let them come to Berlin.

And there are some who say in Europe and elsewhere we can work with the Communists.

—Let them come to Berlin.

And there are even a few who say that it is true that communism is an evil system, but it permits us to make economic progress.

—Lass' sie nach Berlin kommen.

Let them come to Berlin! [6]

Restatement, like repetition, can deepen the impact. It also can add clarity. "Let me put it another way" is a statement that reflects the latter purpose, for restatement is simply the same idea expressed in other words. If the audience missed the meaning the first time around, they are given a second chance. Most of the time they deserve it.

[6] John F. Kennedy, "Ich Bin Ein Berliner," in Aly, *American Short Speeches,* pp. 132-33.

chapter 7

"Let Me Illustrate"

We humans quite often do things the hard way. Much of the time, obviously, it is because we don't know that there is an easier, and possibly better, method available to us. Until someone discovers the wheel we have no choice but to drag heavy things around on a travois.

Yet even when we know that more fruitful courses are there for us to employ, we sometimes ignore them—because they require a bit of initial effort or because we are too proud to use them. Thus we make do with an inefficient hunt-and-peck system of typewriting for 50 years instead of spending the relatively short amount of time it would take to learn typing well enough to double or triple our lifetime output per hour spent at the keyboard. And we try to light our fireplaces without using a sheet or two of rolled up newspaper because an echo of our frontier heritage tells us that that would be cheating.

Both these unproductive human tendencies frequently apply to speechmaking. We struggle to do things entirely with words because we assume that making a visual aid will consume more preparation time than planning and polishing words and phrases—an assumption that may or may not be correct. And we hesitate to use a visual aid because it reminds us a little of the grammar-school activity of "show-and-tell."

"What do you want me to do," the exclamatory question goes, "draw you a picture?" Well, simple, or complicated, as it might appear, that may sometimes be just what you ought to do for your listeners. Draw a picture. Show a diagram. Play a tape recording. Present a few slides. In short, do whatever illustrating is necessary to get your full meaning through to the audience.

That's the real purpose of a visual or aural aid, remember. To help you improve communication—not, as it might appear, to make the speech seem flashier or to keep the drowsier members of the audience awake. The term is almost worn out now, but it remains "visual aid," not "visual gimmick." An illustrative device, whatever it is, has its justification and its utility in helping a message pass from speaker to audience. If this is kept in mind, one will be neither too indifferent nor too proud to draw a picture. Though it may not always be worth 1,000 words, it can in a particular instance be worth quite a bit more.

Think, for example, of the power in a photograph of a young child suffering from the horror of war or the tragedy of famine. How many words would it take you to draw that picture? Or suppose you wish to describe the layout of a data-processing card. Would words alone do the job very thoroughly? And what if you wish to show a group how the ski tow works at a nearby slope? Would not a few sticks and pieces of string serve you better than a dozen paragraphs? I am sure you see the point. Special materials or devices can in fact be aids, not simply gimmicks.

THE FOUR ROLES OF VISUAL AIDS

Basically, the visual aids you call upon have four functions: (1) to represent concrete objects more conveniently or more graphically; (2) to represent nonphysical objects or abstract concepts; (3) to obtain an emotional response; and (4) to reinforce retention or memory.

As to the first function, it includes convenience. The disadvantages of bringing an elephant into the lecture hall are obvious. You wouldn't have much trouble getting attention, but you would have more trouble than I care to contemplate with entryways and ceilings, not to mention with the beast itself. One can extend this example to many other forms of wildlife, and to airplanes, sports cars, sky-scrapers, and other things which belong outside. At the same time, many small objects that would fit tidily in the palm of your hand aren't of much use to you if only the people in the first row can see them in detail. The advantages, then, of using visual aids to represent concrete objects more graphically under certain circumstances are clear. Watch mechanisms, anatomical systems, campus layouts, car designs, battle-field topography, and the like are natural subjects for visual aids. They are too big, too small, too intricate, or too inaccessible to be of much use in and of themselves.

What, however, do I mean when I suggest that visual aids can "represent nonphysical objects or abstract concepts?" Well, in this case I mean things that are there and yet not there. Profit and loss, for in-stance. Or the birth rate. Or the medieval relationship of heaven, hell, and purgatory. Or the ideal table of organization of an army unit. Or a vital scientific theory—any of the numerous "things" that can be much more meaningful when shown graphically.

Even objects that technically are physical or material can fall more or less into this category. Think of the branches of our govern-ment for a moment. Yes, the people filling positions in those branches exist, as do the offices and buildings which house them. But does not the form of the government stand apart from flesh and mortar? It is this nonphysical object that normally we represent by chart or dia-gram, not a set of buildings and their temporary occupants. Consider the absurdity of presenting a model of the innumerable structures and individuals in the Department of State alone and you will see what I mean. Our illustrative devices tend to follow our mental concepts.

Not that they should always do so. Perhaps your talk on govern-ment would be less impersonal if you did think of people and not form. One small office of the State Department might be represented by photos and some family data of the persons who work there. Such an aid could serve as a reminder that "they"—the government—are people, ourselves. Do not overlook this aspect of visual-aid development. As far as is possible, humanize those drawings or charts. Change abstract statistics about auto fatalities to graphic images of the people who died or of the mangled wreckage of the vehicles which carried them to their deaths, and you have illustrations not as easily overlooked as statistics might be.

This leads us to the use of visual or aural aids "to obtain an emotional response," be it sympathy, fear, a sense of well-being, or anger. The actual use and misuse of the emotional response I leave to a later chapter. For the moment let me note, however, that few devices are as effective in this regard as are visual or sound materials. Propagandists know well what a photograph of brutality, real or alleged, can achieve. Without becoming a professional propagandist you can explore the possibilities contained in a picture of a crippled child when you make an appeal for the United Fund, or in a recording of the school fight song when you make an appeal for college spirit. Or in the smell of roasting peanuts when you're asking your fellow students to buy them to raise funds for an important function. There are often better ways to reach the heart or the senses than by spoken words alone.

Naturally you don't wish to turn a speech into a bundle of hokum or to become a modern medicine-show pitchman. Nevertheless, those showmen and the advertising men who succeeded them were successful in large part because of the graphic techniques they employed to play upon human desires. Has any persuasive device been more effective over the years than the before-and-after drawing or photograph? It generates the emotional readiness the salesman needs to pursue his case, in print or in person. Although it is to be hoped that our goals are a step above those of the huckster, we should not, as speakers or listeners, be unaware of the power of the visual aid to strengthen or alter feelings. Jesus, in the incident of the woman taken in adultery (John 8:1-11), reversed the emotional bent of an angry gathering by scratching a visual aid in the sand as he asked who would throw the first stone.

The fourth function I listed for the visual aid was that of increasing retention. If we only hear something it is not as likely to make as lasting an impression as if we hear it and see it. An experienced speaker often will try to make his message stick in the mind by employing avenues of both sight and sound. He uses an aid to let us see what he is talking about, even when it is not very complicated, in order to double his chances of implanting his ideas. Indeed, in some instances he adds sound to sound. He tells us about a unit of music or an emergency warning system, then lets us hear it, the actual sound reinforcing the described one. The use of aids as memory strengtheners is all too often overlooked. In any speech you make, there is a definite possibility that what you say will be remembered better if you add a visual or aural image to your remarks.

KINDS OF AIDS

Our sales message for illustrative aids having been concluded, it is time to offer some suggestions on the various devices and the times to use them. Many of the aids you know about and probably have used —charts, maps, drawings, and the like. But because they can serve different purposes, it is well to look at them individually to see their particular strengths and weaknesses.

Before considering the various aids, though, consider that the most appropriate visual devices may be the actual objects you are describing in your speech. They normally require no special preparation and are logical choices for speeches of demonstration. On the other hand, actual objects, as I have already observed, are not always obtainable or easy to use. That is why it often is necessary to create or improvise other materials. Still, if a tennis racket is the best device for demonstrating follow-through or a human head the best article for demonstrating a new coiffure, don't think it necessary to fashion some artificial apparatus. Visual aids justify their existence only by helping you do something more effectively than you can through other means.

Models

The closest representations of real things, models may serve the purpose of the moment better than the objects they replace. Certainly a model airplane is more convenient for showing an audience the principles of flight than an aircraft ever could be. Models have the additional advantage of being adaptable to cut-away techniques. That is, the outside structure can often be removed to reveal the inner parts or workings. To get to the interior of real objects can be difficult if not impossible. Few if any human beings, for example, would relish being used to provide direct observation of the skeletal or nervous system. One uses, therefore, a model of the human head and neck to show how the speech mechanism functions, disassembling and assembling the parts as one likes with no fear of anguished cries from dissected assistants.

Sometimes it lies within the talents of a speaker to construct his own models, be they close representations or merely rough approximations made of pipe cleaners or clay. A few small poles and a piece of cloth, for instance, can be turned into an excellent table-top device for showing how a sailboat is maneuvered. The talent here is not so much artistic as imaginative. No skill at all is required to convert a collection of marbles, oranges, grapefruits, and rubber balls into a visual aid portraying the size and spatial relationships of the solar system. A classic example of improvisation was the use of Ping Pong balls and mousetraps to present a fanciful demonstration of a nuclear chain reaction.

In some instances a satisfactory model is beyond the capability, financial or creative, of the speaker. These situations generally are ones in which excellent devices already have been fashioned. It is often possible to borrow them. Fire departments, for example, use mannequins for teaching resuscitation (though male speech students seem to prefer coed helpers in demonstrating mouth-to-mouth techniques). Dental offices have large toothbrushes and dentures for instruction in proper brushing. If you borrow, however, use special care in handling the implements. They can be both difficult and expensive to replace.

Graphics

Drawings, photographs, and maps, though not three-dimensional, are representative of real objects and are quite usable when movement or the "feel" of an object is not important. Photographs lend themselves well to emotional appeals and to showing what a statue or building or piece of landscape really looks like. Drawings are effective in showing what the human eye or the camera cannot see and for cut-aways or overlays. Biological lectures and scientific textbooks scarcely can do the job without some sort of pen-and-ink draftsmanship, often in many colors.

No picture is much good, however, if it is not big enough to be seen easily from any part of the room. Nor is it of any value if it is cluttered with detail to the point of being meaningless. This is particularly true of a map. Don't expect to accomplish anything with a service-station road guide, no matter how large it is. Prepare instead a simplified version showing only essential detail.

If step-by-step information is important, as in a presentation on the Bay of Pigs landing or the Battle of Gettysburg, prepare several maps—or use a transparent plastic overlay that lets you draw with a

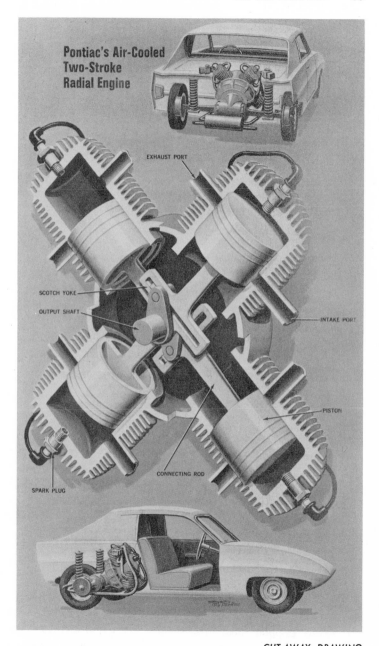

Pontiac's Air-Cooled
Two-Stroke
Radial Engine

EXHAUST PORT

SCOTCH YOKE

OUTPUT SHAFT

INTAKE PORT

PISTON

CONNECTING ROD

SPARK PLUG

CUT-AWAY DRAWING

Reprinted courtesy of Popular Science, and the artist, Ray Pioch.
© 1969 by Popular Science Publishing Co. Inc.

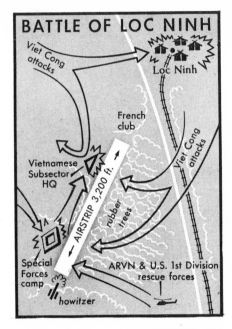

SIMPLIFIED MAP

Reprinted by permission from TIME, The Weekly Newsmagazine;
Copyright Time Inc. 1967.

grease pencil and then rub the markings off. Too many doodlings on one map result in a scrambled forest of arrows and crosses.

You can, of course, make a map three-dimensional by sketching it on a flat surface and building up elevated portions with clay. This increases the physical reality and lets you implant toy soldiers or buildings and change their positions on the terrain. You will have to tilt your contour map, though, to be certain your audience can see it. The alternative is asking people to gather around you, not the most successful practice when the group is large.

Charts, Tables, and Graphs

Most people make little or no distinction between these aids, and assuredly they are of a kind. They are representations of information, the most literal being the type of chart I already have mentioned, the map. Whether you select chart, table, graph, or all of them for a speech depends upon what you have in mind.

For instance, if you wish to show how your club's budget is broken down or what the male-female ratio is like at your college, a pie chart is a good choice. It lets you compare the parts of a whole at a single glance. You can mark off the pieces of the pie without separating them:

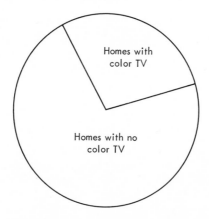

Or you can pull the pieces of the pie apart for greater emphasis.

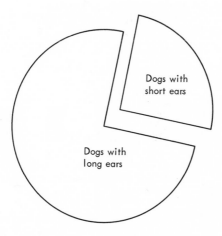

The pie may be cut into more than two pieces and the pieces given different colors for increased comprehension. Be careful, though, of creating so many slices that the portions become slivers. Like a real pie, a visual-aid one can be divided just so far and still satisfy those contemplating it.

When more than four or five segments are in order or when complex information is involved, a bar graph may be appropriate. Half a dozen bars can stand side by side:

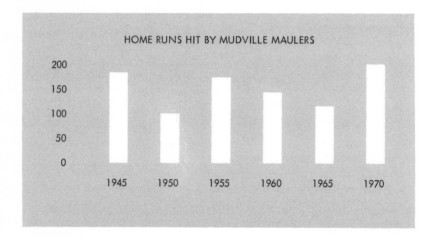

And the bars themselves can be subdivided:

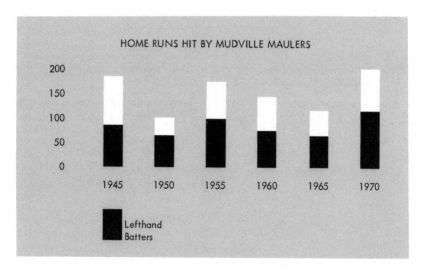

Naturally, the bars can be extended horizontally as well as vertically, and they can be divided into more than two sections. There is real danger, however, in making the graphs too complicated. An aid that looks fine in a textbook may not work at all before an audience. Think of the combination of nearsighted, farsighted, and normal-

U.S. ARMED FORCES AND MEN AVAILABLE FOR CALL-UP

ARMED FORCES 3,398,711

ARMY 1,463,002
NAVY 746,717
MARINES 298,486
AIR FORCE 890,606

SELECTED RESERVE FORCE 150,000

ARMY RESERVE 31,000
NATIONAL GUARD 119,000

The Selected Reserve Force is sufficiently well trained so as to be ready for action in nine to twelve weeks.

RESERVES 2,195,000

ARMY 998,000
NAT'L GUARD 301,000
NAVY 374,000
MARINES 128,000
AIR FORCE 308,000
AIR GUARD 86,000

Ready Reserves receive periodic training, but would require up to nine months to be ready for action.

1A DRAFT POOL 1,396,136

These men are liable to call-up. The Pentagon expects to draft at least 240,000 in the coming year.

PICTOGRAPH   © 1968 by the New York Times Company.   Reprinted by permission.

89

seeing individuals spread about the auditorium or lecture room, none of them able to move toward or away from the aid, and you will see why your graphs or similar visual aids must be kept simple. Also you will recognize why it is important to orient the audience to your aid when you introduce it, and to offer regular reminders of the several parts as you show it. Certainly you will wish to keep the printed material to a minimum. A formal title is not needed if you tell your listeners what the graph shows.

Sometimes, by the way, the aid can almost explain itself. Nothing prevents you from turning a bar graph into a pictograph, that is, into an illustration in which pictures take the place of the bars. An aid to be viewed by an audience from some feet away does not require such precision that it must be laid out to the millimeter. Nor does it require such dignity that a little imagination cannot be employed in making a comparison. On the preceding page is a pictorial equivalent of a bar graph used by the *New York Times* to indicate the size and numerical relationships of our armed forces. It would have to be simplified, of course, for speech purposes.

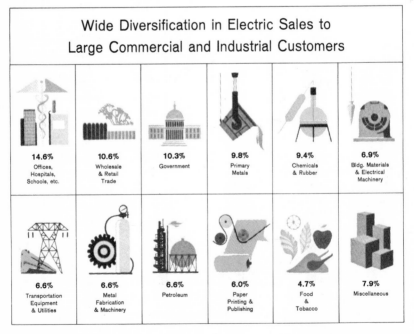

PICTORIAL TABLE

Philadelphia Electric

Pictures can be used to embellish or add definition to many kinds of aids. Opposite, that least dramatic of all illustrations, the statistical table, is arrayed in a bit of fancy dress that reinforces the information presented.

More interesting than a table, and more elastic than a bar graph, is the line graph. The twists and turns of the ascending or descending lines can portray a surprising amount of information:

Strike-Outs Favored Over Walks by 8-5

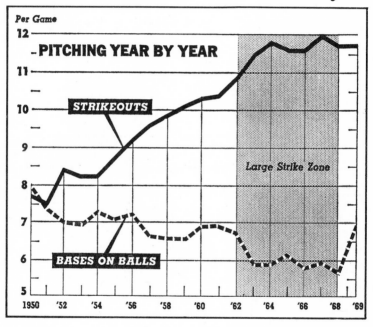

LINE GRAPH
© 1969 by the New York Times Company.
Reprinted by permission.

Remember, though, you can't crowd too much information into your line graph or you will lose more than you gain. The use of different colors or shadings can help measurably.

One of the simplest-to-produce aids in the chart-graph grouping is the *organization chart*. It can portray the multitude of relationships and structures that might be found in business, government bureaus, or military units. It can show who supervises whom, how the chain of command runs, which offices are interrelated, and so on. This chart represents the organizational structure of a college faculty and administration:

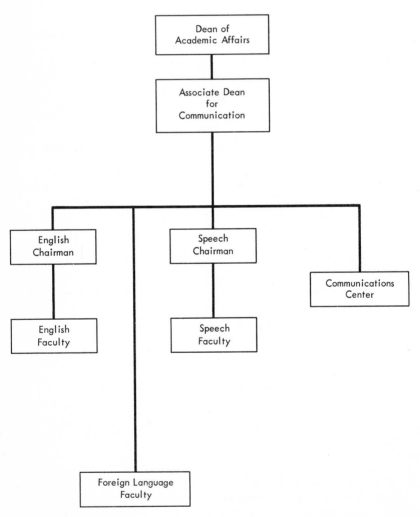

DIVISION OF COMMUNICATION

ORGANIZATION CHART

In organizational charts, lines of authority are normally indicated by solid lines, and cooperative staff relationships by broken lines. No chart, however, can indicate the subtleties that actually exist within an organization—how much authority one officer has over another, how close a relationship is. Therefore, the organizational chart should only be used to approximate a structure, not to represent ultimate truth as carved on stone tablets. Do not place too much emphasis upon what is simply a convenient way of pulling together some otherwise confusing relationships. Like the human beings it represents, the chart could change tomorrow. Your remarks should reflect this possibility, whether you mention it or not.

When the flow of information or material is more important than lines of authority, the pyramidal organizational chart generally gives way to the *flow chart*. This one shows not who is boss, but how educational films start on the way to classrooms:

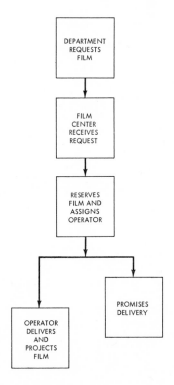

FLOW CHART

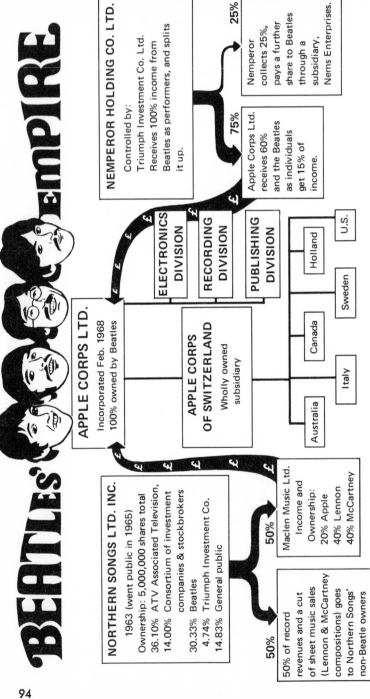

BEATLES' empire

NORTHERN SONGS LTD. INC.

1963 (went public in 1965)
Ownership: 5,000,000 shares total
36.10% ATV Associated Television,
14.00% Consortium of investment
companies & stockbrokers
30.33% Beatles
4.74% Triumph Investment Co.
14.83% General public

50%

50% of record revenues and a cut of sheet music sales (Lennon & McCartney compositions) goes to Northern Songs' non-Beatle owners

50%

Maclen Music Ltd.
Income and Ownership:
20% Apple
40% Lennon
40% McCartney

APPLE CORPS LTD.

Incorporated Feb. 1968
100% owned by Beatles

ELECTRONICS DIVISION

RECORDING DIVISION

PUBLISHING DIVISION

APPLE CORPS OF SWITZERLAND

Wholly owned subsidiary

Australia Italy Canada Sweden Holland U.S.

NEMPEROR HOLDING CO. LTD.

Controlled by:
Triumph Investment Co. Ltd.
Receives 100% income from
Beatles as performers, and splits it up.

75%

Apple Corps Ltd. receives 60% and the Beatles as individuals get 15% of income.

25%

Nemperor collects 25%, pays a further share to Beatles through a subsidiary, Nems Enterprises.

94

A composite of chart and picture is this one by *Time Magazine* artist V. Puglisi, showing the financial empire of some popular entertainers. Do you think there is too much detail for use on a speaking platform?

Chalk and Display Boards

When students are assigned visual-aid talks, the first device most seem to think of is the chalkboard or blackboard. And yet their instructor is quite likely to forbid its use. Why is that? Well, in the first place, he probably wishes them to discover that there are other visual aids. Second, he no doubt recognizes that the chalkboard is one of the more difficult tools to use correctly and effectively.

It takes skill to maintain audience interest when you are facing the opposite way, scratching away at a vertical surface with an untapered writing instrument that can crack or crumble at any moment. You have to write or draw with enough draftsmanship or legibility that your audience can detect your meaning—not an easy job for most humans, who rarely draw or write well, especially while making a speech. Then, you have to make sure that your arm or body does not lie between your audience and what you have drawn or written and that the board itself does not become so filled with scribbling that your visual aid looks like a snowstorm. Finally, you have to be very careful or you will find yourself giving your talk to the board itself.

There are speakers who can use a chalkboard skillfully, their

PICTORIAL ORGANIZATION CHART

markings unfolding the meaning as their tongues speak it, but they are not as numerous as might be hoped. Also, the audiences of the effective chalk-talkers often are highly motivated individuals such as science students or athletic teams. An ordinary audience can be put to sleep rapidly by a blackboard amateur—who can't even see that they are dozing off.

Use a chalkboard if you think it will help you, but don't use it casually. Plan what you are going to do and, if possible, prepare your writings or diagrams on the blackboard before the speech. Your hand will be steadier then, and you can take more time to fashion your zigs and zags. Naturally, you will want to cover the markings—with a hanging movie screen, perhaps—to avoid giving the audience something distracting to look at while you are on another segment of your speech.

A good substitute for a chalkboard is a large writing tablet on an easel. It allows the speaker to partially face the audience even as he writes. The felt pen or grease pencil he uses is more convenient and substantial than a piece of chalk. And he can present his ideas one at a time without having to erase or to spread them all over an array of boards. If only a few sheets are needed, they can be flipped over the top out of the way; if many are needed, it is wiser to tear them off as they are used, dropping them quietly to the floor. The sheets will tear more easily, by the way, if they are perforated or scored lightly beforehand.

Two alternatives to the chalkboard that are coming into greater use in the classroom and lecture hall are the *magnetic board* and the *flannel board or felt board*. Both employ prepared aids which are attached lightly to the display board in advance of or during the speech. Plastic magnetic tape will hold a piece of visual material to a metal surface or magnetic chalkboard. A small backing of flannel or some sticky tape will cause small cards or pictures to adhere to the felt board, which is simply a piece of flannel or felt stretched upon a frame.

The materials used with these devices can be made by the speaker or cut from magazines or pamphlets. They can be words, sentences, pictures of trees or people, almost anything that can be drawn or printed. With a magnetic board they can even be small objects, such as chessmen or miniature footballs and players. The familiar chalk talk takes on a third dimension with these kinds of visual aids, which allow all the players to be moved to the positions they would occupy at any point in a play. Certainly it's a lot more vivid than a flock of X's and O's.

The special boards lend themselves well to analysis or synthesis. You can take your subject apart or put it together before the eyes of the audience. Suppose, for example, you are describing the basic instrument groups of an orchestra—the strings, the brass, the woodwinds, and so on. You might present a picture of a full orchestra and point to the various sections as you talk about them. But the various parts will not stand out as strongly and individually as they would if you were to place representations of them on a display board one at a time, talking about each as you go along. Your listener would then meet each new section singly and have the opportunity to become acquainted with it before he is confronted with the next part. His thinking mechanism has a little better chance to do its job. So does his memory. This same principle holds true if you are explaining how a rifle is stripped down for a cleaning or how to get to the insides of a sewing machine. For step-at-a-time demonstrations, a simple flannel board may be unsurpassed. It works well with a lesson on the latest dance step or one on how to set the table for polite society.

Optical Devices

The *lens-and-lamp* devices most commonly used by speakers to throw an enlarged image on a screen are the four basic projectors: slide, film, overhead, and opaque.

The *opaque* requires the least advance preparation, in that it will accept almost any object that will fit on its display surface, from photographs, clippings, and books to stamps, coins, and shells. The disadvantage of the opaque projector, aside from the noise and heat it generates, is that it is necessary to darken the room to a degree comparable to that for showing movies. The speaker can't see his notes or his audience very well, and he has to do a careful job of placing the object under the gate so that it will be oriented properly on the screen. Some speakers also object to the bulk of the instrument, particularly if they have to move it from place to place.

Slide projectors, far more common than opaque projectors, are small enough to be transported easily and can be operated in an only slightly darkened room. One compact tray can hold several dozen slides, whose subject matter may be photographs of places and people or of charts, tables, maps, and models. The speaker can take the pictures himself if he has a little photographic skill, or he can borrow or buy them.

Using slides in a lecture is not as easy as it might appear, however. Obviously the slides must be placed in the proper sequence and inserted carefully into the tray so that they appear right side up on the screen. The screen and the projector must be stationed in positions that allow the audience to see the projected images without blocking the throw of light. And the speaker must determine where he will stand—beside the instrument, as he would with an opaque projector, or in front of the group, assuming he has a remote control attachment or a projectionist assistant.

Facing the audience, even in a darkened room, has obvious advantages. Do so whenever you can. Naturally, you'll need some cueing arrangements if you are working with a helper. Clicking gadgets are sometimes used, as are small flashlight signals. Quite often, though, you can tell your assistant that a change is in order simply by pausing slightly. Oh, yes, you could say each time, "Now in our next slide . . . ," but that gets terribly repetitious and actually leads to a monotonous presentation because it becomes the only means of transition. Always know, or have on your outline, what the next slide portrays. This way you can lead into it in a manner that varies a little. Sometimes it is nice to take the audience a bit by surprise by not saying too much before the image appears.

A word of caution here about slide projectors. Despite the claims of their manufacturers, they are singularly unreliable when counted upon most. Possibly the machines are shy before groups, because it is a rare presentation in which at least one slide doesn't jam. Anticipate this situation, therefore, and don't be stunned when it happens. When using any mechanical device, in fact, have a plan to fall back on if nothing works or if things break down halfway through. These are extreme situations, of course, but if you are ready for them, one jammed slide will seem to be a minor matter.

What can you do in anticipation of mechanical failure? Check things out in advance, for one thing. Make sure that the wall outlet has power, that the tray fits the projector, that no slide has somehow gotten out of order or upside down. A quick runthrough before the audience arrives is always comforting if you can manage it. And once you have had that first projection lamp, or bulb, burn out during your remarks you will never try another slide presentation without carrying an extra lamp in your pocket or purse, or without making sure that one has been placed on the projection table by your host.

If I make it seem perilous to do a slide talk, I am only revealing the often sad truth. The potential of the slide projector is great, yet so is the risk if precautions are not taken. And even then, absolute smoothness cannot be assured. Until you have acquired some skill as a speaker, until you have become more or less imperturbable, it might be wise to avoid slide presentations and employ more reliable visual aids.

Film projectors are not used very often by the ordinary speaker, but they can be useful in adding movement and perspective to a talk. Like slides, films can be homemade, bought, or borrowed. They portray motion as no other artificial aid except a model can, and they are relatively convenient to handle. Unless you plan to turn your talk into a travelog or documentary, however, you probably won't use film within a speech to the extent you would use slides. Movies have a way of taking over and making other things appear anticlimactic. If you employ a film, sound or silent, don't let it become a crutch that you quickly introduce and then answer questions about afterward. A speech should contain all the essential elements of organization and presentation whether or not a film is part of it. The film should have its proper moment on the stage and no more.

There is a medium that lies between motion picture and slide. It is the *film strip*, a series of still pictures on a reel of film. Although it is a good educational tool, you are not as likely to have the facilities for making a film strip as you are for a motion picture or set of slides. Film strips may be used with recorded sound tracks, or live narration may be added as they are shown. If you are the narrator you should know what is coming next, just as you should when showing a motion picture or using the slide projector. With a motion picture, need I add, the pacing of the images is generally out of your hands while the projector is running. To narrate, you have to know your material well or be adept at handling a scripted narration while the film plays.

A projection device that is being used increasingly is the *overhead projector*. Usable in an undarkened room, it also permits the speaker to face his audience while operating it. The materials of the overhead projector are transparencies closer in size to typewriter paper than they are to the 2- by 2-inch inserts of the slide projector. Most colleges and libraries, and many offices, have equipment for making transparencies at nominal cost.

In the photograph below an ambitious instructor uses two overhead projectors in the same lesson.

Photograph by Thomas A. Michener.

As a speaker you might find it convenient to use an overhead projector in a particular talk. If pointing out specific parts of a list, table, or diagram is important, you need not turn away from your audience or handle a large pointer. You need only touch the tip of your pencil to the appropriate part of the transparency and the indication will appear on the screen behind you. When interior-exterior relationships or special sequences are significant, you can put one transparency on top of one or more others (or reverse the process) and have kingsize overlays. An additional advantage of many overhead projectors is a roller attachment which permits you to write on a transparent substance with pen or grease pencil as you go along. It is better than using a chalkboard in that you continue to face the audience while writing words of a size you are accustomed to. You can, of course, draw or write on any transparency without harming it by placing a clear overlay on top. Your markings can be wiped off later if you use a grease pencil.

REVIEW AND SUGGESTIONS

I have presented you with a variety of ways for enhancing your talks with visual materials—and mentioned the value of aural aids such as phonograph records or tapes as well. While aids to the ear generally are associated with specialized subjects—musical analyses, bird songs, Morse code, and the like—you may have a speech in which you can use them, perhaps to create an emotional mood or to supplement a bit of dance instruction. We can only hope that you will take advantage of the several means available to you for representing concrete objects, for representing nonconcrete objects or abstract concepts, for achieving an emotional response, or for reinforcing memory.

Because using special aids may be a new experience for you, there follow, in one package, a few general rules for handling illustrative devices. Some I have mentioned already, others are new. Most apply to a variety of aids, from chalkboard to slide projector. First, the "do's."

1. Test the visibility (or the audibility) of your aids by taking a seat in the rear of the lecture room, or at a comparable distance from the object in another place.

2. Keep the aid out of sight, if at all possible, until you are ready to use it. Why give the audience something possibly more interesting than your smiling face to look at?

3. As soon as you are through with the aid, put it away.

4. Use a pointer—even a yardstick—to direct your audience's eyes to specific areas. Without a pointer you'll have to work too close to the aid, blocking parts of it with your hand or arm.

5. If possible, keep the aid before you, or at least beside you. When you need to give your audience information, it is better to put your reminders into your notes or on the back of a chart than to twist your head and body around and read them from the aid itself.

6. Make the aids move internally. Assemble. Take apart. Slide the line across the graph. Uncover. Unroll. Unfold.

7. Let color help you add interest, definition, meaning. Remember the conventional associations, however. Audiences can be confused by red grass, green stoplights, orange oceans.

Now the "don'ts":

1. Don't try to hold a bulky aid, or one as flimsy as tissue paper. Rest aids like these on something steadier than your hands can be. Make sure the sight lines remain good, though.

2. If it is necessary to hold an object, don't wave it through the air or fiddle with it distractedly.

3. Don't put too much information on a single aid. It just gives the audience something to read or stare at as you talk of something else.

4. Don't distribute or have the audience circulate materials while you speak. Audiences will read anything you give them in preference to listening, and letting them pass items about creates distractions. If there is no other way, however, read the printed material along with the audience and make no attempt to present complicated information while objects are going from hand to hand.

5. Don't let a visual aid, no matter how unusual, hypnotize you. Talk to your audience, not to the object. No warning is violated more than this one. Sometimes whole speeches are given to bowling balls.

6. Don't take all your cues from the visual aid. Lead it, don't let it lead you. Vary your transitions by knowing what is coming next. Audiences grow weary of too many repetitions of "Now in our next chart . . ."

I hope these suggestions will help you to plan and present visual aids as effectively as possible. Add these support materials to your speeches whenever you find that they are appropriate and useful. With each employment of them your over-all presentation will improve.

PRESENTATION

chapter 8

The Delivery

Now that you have learned about some of the essentials in preparing a speech, it is time to consider how to deliver it. But before I discuss techniques of delivery, let me emphasize that they are just that—techniques—methods by which technical details are treated. Delivery is not the heart of the matter; it is the external means of revealing that heart. It is the way in which the speaker transfers his meaning to the listener. Good delivery is important to the communication process, it's true; nevertheless, it remains merely a manner of carrying a message.

In days past, this fact often got lost. The presentation process seemed to be the important thing. Speakers waved their arms in gigantic gestures, let their words roll over the countryside like elegant whitecaps, gazed at an angry or benign heaven, and paused in Napoleonic posture to survey their apparent handiwork. Each trilled accent was polished to high luster, each gesture planned with the care involved in executing a double reverse on the gridiron. Nothing was left to chance except the message itself, for impression was more important than meaning.

At the beginning of this century William Jennings Bryan, who three times ran for the Presidency, was considered a master of oratory. Indeed, he won his first nomination in large part because of his Cross of Gold speech at the Democratic convention. Bryan's speeches were punctuated with applause from beginning to end. When he finished one, more than a few of his hearers exclaimed, "Wasn't that magnificent!" And in a way, these people were right. Bryan's speeches were spectacular. But they also bore a certain resemblance to Chinese dinners. An hour or so later, they weren't very satisfying. In fact, following one of Bryan's roaringly cheered orations Governor Altgeld of Illinois said in bewilderment, "I have been thinking over Bryan's speech. What did he say, anyhow?" [1]

Now, was that speech a success or not? Yes, if one views it from the standpoint of conveying emotion to an audience. No, if one considers it important that the audience know what the speaker said or carry away with it some meaning from the moments spent in listening. Naturally, no one wishes to hear a speaker who is cold and emotionless. At the same time, no one gets any lasting value from bombast for its own sake. It is ironic yet understandable that Bryan, a sincere man for all his oratorical flourishes, is remembered less than positively for what in his lifetime represented his greatest triumphs—speeches which now seem as significant and meaningful as a compact sermon by Batman to Robin. The Great Commoner was almost foretelling his fate when he told one audience, "I want to talk to your hearts. I found out a long time ago that talking to men's heads don't count."

It is not that what was said to another generation can have no meaning today. The speeches by Lincoln stand as eternal evidence to refute such an idea. It is simply that speakers who emphasize delivery above everything else are remembered precisely for their emphasis, not for what they said.

Is there, then, any value in giving any attention to your delivery? Of course there is. Just as there is in selecting the right accessory to accent your attire, or in using punctuation marks in something you write, or in deciding whether you will send your message by letter instead of making a telephone call. Effective delivery is part planning, part practice, and part experience.

First of all you have to decide what basic method of presentation you will use. Will you memorize your speech? Will you read it? Will you speak from an outline and notes? Thus far, the suggestions

[1] Ray Ginger, *Six Days or Forever?* (New York: The New American Library Inc., 1960), p. 27. The remark was made to Clarence Darrow.

presented in this book have been flexible. But about memorization I feel strongly. Unless you are an experienced theatrical performer or one speaker in a million, I advise you to stay away from the fully memorized speech.

THE DISADVANTAGES
OF THE MEMORIZED SPEECH

There is nothing at all wrong with committing to memory a few key sentences if you're speaking from notes or from a manuscript. Memorizing an entire speech, on the other hand, has some real disadvantages. The most obvious one is the danger of *going blank.* Few situations are more painful for speaker and audience than that in which the man or woman at the lectern stares with anguished eye at a roomful of uncomfortably squirming individuals who are hoping as strongly as the speaker that the lost words will come back before another second passes.

This dreaded and inevitable blacking out occurs because the speaker reciting from memory is not really thinking. He is only saying words. He is little more than a living, breathing phonograph playing back the bit of sound that was put on the turntable sometime earlier. And because his thinking processes have been bypassed, he is as helpless as a short-circuited phonograph when something goes wrong. In a manner of speaking, he too has been short-circuited. He can't work his way out of the hole because, on a reasoning level, he doesn't know what he has been talking about. All he can do is to put the mental needle back into an earlier groove and try again.

The same mental set or lack of it that causes a speaker to forget his carefully polished phrases also results in another weakness of the memorized speech: *inflexibility.* The speech reciter can't react intelligently to developments of the moment because his chief hope is to keep on going. One break and he's in trouble. Thus he ignores the important remark made just before his presentation, and by so doing makes his audience wonder if he might have been sleeping for the hour preceding his speech. Only the most poised and experienced speaker can blend the memorized and the impromptu without appearing awkward or letting the interpolations throw him off the track.

And only the poised and experienced speaker with *theatrical presence* can make a memorized speech not sound like one. Our record-player comparison comes back again. Often the most fitting sign-off to a canned speech would be: "This has been a recording." Even those memorized speeches which abound in inflection and gesture tend to have an air of phoniness about them. They seem too good to be true.

A BETTER WAY

It must be obvious from all this that I recommend either the written or the extemporaneous speech over the memorized one. But which form do I like most? As a general rule, the *extemporaneous*. And please don't confuse this with impromptu, or ad lib, speech. Unlike the *impromptu* presentation, which is delivered off-the-cuff, without preparation, the extemporaneous speech is definitely prepared in advance. The speaker approaches his subject as I have indicated in earlier chapters, prepares a strong outline, and uses it to unfold his remarks. To aid him, he usually has a set of notes, but he does not read his speech. He uses the notes to keep himself on his planned path and to record precisely the quotations, key sentences, or statistics he will use.

Far from being a reciter of pre-set phrases, the extemporaneous speaker is an individual who is *constantly aware of what he is saying—* even though some of the sentences are not quite the pretty sayings they might be if he had set down every word. The extemporaneous speaker is on top of his speech, his remarks give an impression of freshness and spontaneity, and he is ready to adjust them to the situation at any time. That's because he is using his full thought processes as he speaks, not just those necessary for recall. And he need fear no break in a parrotlike flow of words. He is selecting his phrases as he goes along instead of trying desperately to remember them. Compared with the user of the memorized speech, the person speaking extemporaneously enjoys enormous freedom.

What about those *notes* he uses? What should they be like? Above all, speaking notes should be concise. They should be no longer than necessary for the speech of the moment. If they get too lengthy or detailed they become a complete manuscript—and do the speaker more harm than good.

Think of a set of notes as you might a homemade road map designed for quick examination by you or a friend while traveling.

Certain things you will want to indicate exactly and without mistake —turning points, numbers, guide markers. But though you may be well aware that certain things of interest lie along the route, you don't clutter your map with them. They'll only get in the way, making it harder to find the important things.

The *exact form of speaking notes* is something of a personal choice. Some people like to note down only key words or phrases from their outline; others will use whole sentences. I suggest that whatever you put onto paper be set down neatly enough for easy recognition under the pressure of a speaking situation. Scribblings on the back of an envelope can seem a dramatic touch, but they also are hard to read in the less-than-perfect lighting or physical conditions you may encounter on the platform. Typing might make words easier to read, yet many people do better with hand-printed or written notes because the characters can be made larger.

Should you put your notes on *cards or paper?* Again it is a personal choice. Cards generally are easier to handle, on lectern or in hand. Further, they don't rattle or flutter in a slight draft. Nonetheless, they can get mixed up. So number them clearly. And if you use several cards, be sure your speech doesn't get ahead of them. If you forget to flip them as you go along, the wrong card will be on top when you need help. Then you'll have to search for the right one.

A piece of good typing paper will, of course, take more words than a 3 by 5- or 4 by 6-inch index card. Fewer individual pages, therefore, are necessary, thus minimizing the mechanical problems of flipping or turning. Still, the flimsiness of paper leads many lecturers to find a compromise in large note cards, which aren't subject to small changes in air currents, don't crackle, and can be used on both sides without danger that the words from the underside will bleed through.

READING FROM A MANUSCRIPT

Despite the many advantages inherent in the extemporaneous speech because of its flexibility and informality, there are times when it is appropriate for a speaker to read his remarks. *Representatives of governments* find it desirable to do so when any variation in the carefully worked-out statement could cause complications or embarrassment. *Business or labor leaders* might choose to use a manuscript for the same reason. And then, some *experienced lecturers* write out many addresses or sermons for later publishing. They are, however, usually competent extemporaneous speakers and can switch over at any point without encountering the difficulty a beginning speaker would run into were he to intermix techniques.

There are, moreover, *special situations* which may call for a written speech. *Dedications and memorials* lend themselves to a more poetic or philosophical expression than an extemporaneous presentation is likely to contain. The *eulogy* is also read quite often—in order that the sentiments can be as meaningful as possible to the bereaved and because the speaker himself is often too choked with emotion to rely upon finding the right phrases while he is speaking. The moving statements at the services for President John Kennedy and his brother Robert come to mind as examples of the written speech softening thoughts of tragedy that can tear at the mind.

When reading a speech, the speaker must take pains to *avoid a mechanical delivery*. The same holds true, of course, if he reads a long passage within an extemporaneous speech. Reading can become a barrier to communication if it is not carried out in careful manner. It is not as direct as speaking, remember. Things such as basic reading ability, oral inflection, and eye contact become more critically important when a printed page is placed between the speaker and his hearers. The goal is to eliminate or at least to reduce the size of the barrier.

It goes without saying that the person who reads to an audience must *be aware of the meaning* of what he reads. If he's written it himself, that should be no problem—though by failing to practice his presentation he can give the impression of not knowing what he's talking about. If the words are written by another, as in a long extract from a book or article, the speaker must determine the writer's message before he can expect to communicate it to others.

So, meaning comes first, then the techniques of conveying it effectively. Among them is *vocal variety*. People reading aloud tend to fall into annoying patterns of inflection—or use none at all. Those in the latter category speak in the familiar monotone, rarely changing the note on which they utter every syllable. Just as every word should not have the same volume, every word should not be pronounced at the same note on the scale.

Even those who are not monotones can sound a bit wearying after a time, particularly if they have a singsong delivery or, as so often happens, drop their inflections at the end of every sentence:

Duh-DUH-duh-DUH-duh-d
                    u
                     h
                      h.

Duh-DUH-duh-DUH-duh-d
                    u
                     h
                      h.

Duh-DUH-duh-DUH-duh-d
                    u
                     h
                      h.

If you plan to read a speech or a passage, *discover the words that should have emphasis*. Words or phrases can be stressed by being said louder or softer than others; by being placed at a higher pitch or a lower one; by being said briskly or slowly. Analyze your presentation with this in mind. When you decide what words or phrases need special treatment, mark them in a way that will remind you of this once you are before an audience. For most people underlining works well, but consider other signs. An arrow ↗ above a word could mean "raise the pitch"; one below͵ could mean "lower it." Some speakers use capital letters for words that need more VOLUME. And sometimes they place three dots before words that should be preceded by . . . a pause. We caution you not to write "pause" or "louder." Under pressure you just might read that word along with the others: "This is not a time for talk; it is a time for *louder* deliberation."

Without burying yourself in symbols, try to come up with a few that will work for you. It may take a few practice readings for you to become comfortable with them, and you may throw out some and add new ones. But by attempting to gain some vocal variety, you will be performing an act of mercy to those who must listen to you.

One of the real problems of reading to an audience lies in maintaining *eye contact*. Not that it's unimportant in an extemporaneous speech. At all times you can add to the immediacy of the communication by looking at your hearers rather than at the floor or the ceiling or out the window. But to deliver a written speech you have to look at your manuscript part of the time. If you look at it all the time, needless to say, you will seem to be ignoring your audience—and they might respond by ignoring you.

Speakers who do manage to raise their eyes to regard their listeners often have the unfortunate habit of looking up briefly at the beginning of a sentence, then burying their heads in their scripts for the remainder. To see that even professionals do this, watch a few newsmen on television. Unless they have a Teleprompter, they can be expected to look at the camera for the first few words of a sentence and at their scripts for the end. Admittedly, it's necessary to check the pages often enough to get the words right. The trick is in not looking down too long or at the wrong moment.

Frequently, the most important part of a sentence comes at the end—the very time most readers are looking away from instead of at the audience. How can you avoid this weakening of your presentation? One way is by *marking your page* in a way that reminds you to look up. Underlining, if you don't use it for other purposes, might be your method. Or you might use a marking pen that highlights words without covering them.

Another thing you can do is make a conscious effort to *look at your audience as long as you can,* especially at the ends of sentences. This will mean taking in as many words as possible at one glance and having the courage not to look down till you have said them. Frequently speakers consult their scripts more than they really need to. They look at the audience while saying "The United States," then look down as they say "of America." Now those last two words are not any surprise to them. It's not going to turn out to be The United States of Lower Hoboken. The person who returns to his script for "of America" is actually doing so to pick up the words that follow. He could just as well wait till he's said the whole phrase he knows.

Why doesn't he do so? Habit, for one thing. Lack of confidence in his ability to find his place, for another. If you would like to break the habit, practice holding your eyes on an imaginary audience while saying as much of a sentence as you can. You'll be amazed how much longer you can maintain eye contact. And to reduce your apprehension about losing your place, consider some *aids to the eye.* A little period sign . isn't easy to spot while you're reading aloud. But two slashing lines // are easy-to-spot indications of a sentence ending. And one slashing line / is a good way of indicating a pause. Successful announcers use marks like these to improve their delivery. You might find them helpful, too.

Incidentally, for significant changes of thought or mood, as might come at the end of a paragraph or a passage, three slashing lines / / / are sometimes used. They can serve as a warning not to seem too light or too gloomy or too casual at the beginning of the next line. Continuation in the same general mood can be highly inappropriate on occasion. That's why some reminder to shift gears might be beneficial. Newscasters face the problem all the time. If they're not careful, they'll boom into an account of a tragedy with the same lightheartedness they used on a preceding item about a White House wedding. Perhaps you have caught them doing so.

Handling the Manuscript

While considering the problems of reading from a manuscript we should not overlook those of housing and handling it. It might seem enough to type or write your remarks on some sheets of plain paper and carry them with you to the lectern. But how are you going to keep them from getting dog-eared before you use them? And how will you keep the pages from getting mixed up? I once heard a speaker read a speech completely out of order without the audience seeming to notice, but I must say that it wasn't much of a speech before, during, or after delivery.

I strongly recommend, then, that instead of leaving things to providence, you *consider fastening your script within some sort of cover.* It will keep the pages in order, even if you are outside on a windy day. It will keep your masterpiece from getting frayed, rolled, or folded. And it will let you handle your pages comfortably and inconspicuously while you are speaking. *A ring binder* is especially helpful. Standard size typing paper can be inserted, the pages being turned from left to right. At other times 5 by 8-inch note cards can be employed, the speaker flipping them up as he finishes each page.

In handling the manuscript, as in all things related to delivery, find the techniques or devices that are most comfortable for you. *Do a little experimenting* to discover them. You'll find a good working pattern before too long. Your effort to find it will, in the meantime, make you much more aware of the various aspects of delivery. This in itself will result in gradual improvements you might not realize you are making.

chapter 9

Style and Precision

The last chapter dealt with problems related to delivering a speech. But one important aspect of this process was not touched upon—diction. By "diction" two things are meant: *the selection of words and the enunciation of them*. As a speaker you will have to make judgments in both areas.

One judgment I hope you will make is to *avoid slang*. Such expression has its place, but rarely is that place the speaker's platform. Yes, a few prominent speakers occasionally use informal language for special effect or emphasis. Their reputations as masters of spoken language are secure, however. If slang or irregular grammar works for them it is because everyone is aware that they are using the common phrases for a special purpose, not because they do not know any better. Further, such speakers never confuse a touch of seasoning with a whole meal of salt.

Don't assume, though, that because I advise against including language that is not universally acceptable I am urging that your sentences sound fresh from a computer programed to produce uniformity. *Your speech should reflect your personality*. Shaped rather than restricted by the guidelines of accepted grammar, the words you use must seem right coming from your mouth. Are you, for example, the kind of person who would say:

> Having spoken of the influence of the different groups of faculties in leading off and exerting influence, and laying the foundation of success, in different persons, we come now to consider how the different faculties in each of the groups may give shading and peculiarity to the character . . . ?

I doubt very much that you would talk like that. Not only is the statement almost meaningless because of its complicated phraseology, it also sounds pretentious. Unless you desire to appear both cryptic and ultrasophisticated, you won't arrange your words that way for a speech. Even if you did, you would have to possess quite a professional air to get away with such nonsense. The quote is from a nineteenth-century phrenologist—a fellow who studied character and personality by examining bumps on the head.[1]

Suppose we took something a little less peculiar, though. Would these words fit you?

> Relying, then, on the patronage of your good will, I advance with obedience to the work, ready to retire from it whenever you become sensible how much better choice it is in your power to make.

Again, I doubt if you would be comfortable with the word styling quoted. But Thomas Jefferson was. He used this language in his first Inaugural Address, a speech which he did not actually deliver, but sent to Congress to be read. Jefferson's phrasings are not complicated or overblown. They simply don't fit the average American —which Jefferson, most assuredly, was not. Though not artificial coming from him, the words would very likely seem so if uttered by most of the citizens of his nation, present and past.

I suggest, then: Within the framework of accepted grammar *select the words that are natural to you, and arrange them in a manner that is equally natural.* For instance, have you ever heard anyone say, "Coming to the clearing, I saw a campfire burning brightly"? That statement might get by on the printed page—though even there it is

---

[1] Nelson Sizer and H. S. Drayton, *Heads and Faces and How to Study Them* (New York: Fowler and Wells Co., 1895), p. 120.

stilted—but in oral form it just doesn't sound right. The "Entering the room, I discovered three people waiting" construction is both old-fashioned and unnatural. Compare it with "When I came into the room, I found three people waiting." Which arrangement of words sounds better? The latter, I hope. As you plan or deliver your speeches, try to use the normal patterns of speaking, not those of an old-fashioned romantic novel. Avoid fancy phrasing and beware of dragging in too many adjectives.

And *be especially watchful for jargon.* If you are close to a particular subject—a profession, a trade, a hobby—you are likely to begin using words or phrases that are understood only by those in the know. To outsiders they are meaningless. For example, to those familiar with the insides of cars, the words "cam" and "torque" are not unusual. Neither are they items of slang. But to those who don't know the subject, the terms are mysteries. You can't throw them at a general audience without supplying a word of explanation or definition. Otherwise you will lose listeners fast. How can people follow you if they don't know what you're talking about?

When possible, therefore, steer away from the technical language of a subject, be it water-skiing or drag racing. That is, of course, unless you are speaking to a group of specialists or hobbyists. When the technical terms can't be avoided, take a few moments to make sure your audience understands them before you go on. Those moments will be well spent.

There is a second kind of jargon, by the way, which has no justification under any circumstances. Some groups or professions have adopted a set of words and phrases which, unlike "cam" or "torque," do not ordinarily contribute one whit to the improvement of communication with any audience. A generation ago kids spoofed this kind of phoniness when they spouted:

> Do not prognosticate the enumeration of juvenile poultry prior
> to the conclusion of the incubation period.

The kids saw the absurdity of using this language to say, "Don't count your chickens before they hatch," yet a lot of adults still talk like that in the mistaken idea that it improves the message. Sociologists and lawyers bear the greatest weight of criticism for the wholesale adoption of jargon, but the guilt can easily be spread to educators, government workers, business executives, and military personnel.

You don't have to go to many professional or educational meetings before running into more than your share of words such as "methodology," "dichotomy," "parameter," "causative," "core-curriculum," "milieu," "mode," and "strata." Now, there's nothing incorrect in these terms. At times they may be the best ones to use. But is it wise to load your presentation with them? And what is the justification for using them if simpler words will do? If your argument isn't impressive when stated in understandable language, what can you hope to gain by making it harder to comprehend? You might fool a few people into thinking you're a new Einstein. But count on others to see through the fancy spats to the cheap pair of socks underneath.

If you have a good argument, why spoil it by using big words for their own sake? When you mean to tell your audience that you are going to cut a straight line into two parts, don't say, "Now I shall bifurcate the continuum." Is anything accomplished by such nonsense? Instead of looking for the grand term, look for the simple, direct one. When you're tempted to use "initiate," substitute "begin" or "start." In place of "areas of impoverishment," try "slums." If something is coming to a close, let it "end," not "terminate." Chances are that the words that come first to mind are the best for your purpose, so don't struggle to find less natural ones. If you discover that you're quite cozy with words like "bifurcate" and "dichotomy," there's still time to reform; if not, a career awaits you writing income tax forms or instructions for assembling toys.

In selecting and arranging the language of your speech, keep in mind that the words formed by your tongue must reach the listener's mind through his ear, not his eye. A book reader can move at his own pace, stop to look up a difficult word, repeat a line or paragraph as is necessary to gain the meaning. A listener, in contrast, is stuck with what you are saying. He can't slow you down. He has no opportunity to check the meaning of a word. He can't rewind you to an earlier point in your remarks. Don't make his job harder by complicating your language.

And *don't slip into silly patterns built upon extra words.* People used to say, "A penny saved is a penny earned." Now they dress it up: "Money-wise," they remark, "a penny accumulated saving-wise is equivalent to a penny accumulated earning-wise." Ironically, the "-wise" words are just about the most foolish things you can find—language-wise, that is.

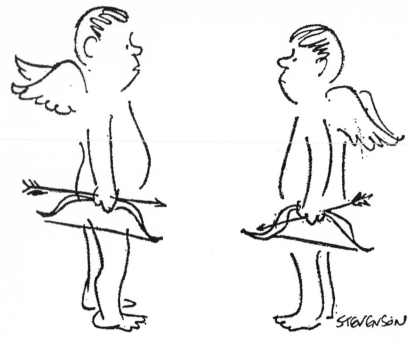

*"Last month, I was concentrating on random attach-
ments of the head-over-heels variety, but this month
I'm utilizing societal and psychological factors in an
attempt to initiate deeper, more meaningful relationships."*

Drawing by Stevenson; © 1969 The New Yorker Magazine, Inc.

More common, though, are the belt-and-suspenders phrases.
These are the ones the speaker uses on the theory, apparently, that
he needs something extra to hold his sentences up. Every eight words
he pauses to say, "You know," never waiting to see if you do or don't,
and not even aware that he inserted the two words in an otherwise
effective sentence. A good "you-knower" can stick two or possibly
three of these little sentence-wreckers into a single statement. He even
learns to bob his head while doing so, distracting his listeners that
much more. Variations or additions he may include in his repertoire are
"you see," "and everything," "if you will," and "let me say."

On the barest chance that you might be a "you-knower," I
wish to assure you that all is not lost. You can defeat the habit with a
bit of effort. The same goes for the frequent use of "uh" between
thoughts, or of "so" at the beginning of them. Sometimes these habits
creep in because a person is afraid of a pause. This is unfortunate
because pauses can be effective. Certainly they are better than a

string of "uh-h-h-h-s." But if you set aside your fear of the pause and still go on saying "you know" or "uh," recognize that by being aware of your problem you are halfway home. It's the unaware "uh-er" who doesn't get saved.

As you speak, try to catch yourself in your particular foible. You might spoil a sentence or two, but eventually you'll become your own policeman. If you're not sure which habit is the culprit, ask a friend to help you. He'll let you know what to look out for. If you like, he'll keep score. With each speech the number of waste phrases or sounds will go down. After a few rounds of speaking they should be at a respectable minimum.

Don't expect perfection, by the way. No one really attains it. What's more, an occasional "uh" can add naturalness to the delivery. I remember when network broadcast engineers and editors discovered that by editing audio tape they could cut out every flaw in a speaker's presentation. The result was an artificial delivery that seemed too good to be true. The engineers soon went back to a less severe editing and speakers sounded human again.

Enough of word selection, intentional or otherwise. The next thing to consider is diction in the sense of pronunciation. By this time of life you surely have had more than your fill of people telling you to say things correctly. At the risk of being just one more, your author has to certify that *correct pronunciation and good articulation* are important to a successful speech.

Why? Well think about it for a minute. Oh yes, it's nice to possess diction that a precisionist such as Henry Higgins, in George Bernard Shaw's *Pygmalion,* could approve of—the perfect pronunciation of "The rain in Spain falls mainly in the plain." But we don't speak primarily to please precisionists, do we? We speak to get a message through to our listeners. We hope that they will understand as much as possible of what we say. It follows, then, that we should want to pronounce our words carefully and as close to the generally agreed-upon pattern as we can.

Notice that I didn't say "pronounce our words as the dictionary tells us." Dictionaries don't really tell people how to say things. Dictionaries merely record the pronunciations that at a given time are considered standard, that is, those that are used by most educated people of a nation or region. In other words, instead of dictionaries telling people, people tell dictionaries. Professional linguists try to make good judgments in recording pronunciations for inclusion in dictionaries, but their decisions are rooted in usage. Remember that. When you look up a word, you are getting the benefit of careful thinking and observation that will help you reach your audience more effectively—either by saying the word in a manner most understandable to those listening to you or by avoiding a glaring mispronunciation that causes your hearers to lose confidence in you. Never underestimate the power of a pronunciation boner to make those in an audience chuckle, or scratch their heads in confusion, or wonder why they should pay much attention to someone who doesn't even know how to say the words he picked for his own speech.

Now, for most pronunciations you don't have to go to a dictionary—or at least you think you don't have to. By the time you reach adulthood you have mastered the proper sounding of thousands of words. The problem in speaking is to remember to say them as well as you know how. You have to avoid dropping carelessly the final "g" in "-ing" words—"singing," "running," "walking," "laughing"—words you use many times each day. You have to remember that the first letter of "just" is "j" and the second one "u"; otherwise, you will come up with "jist" or "dist" or "dust" or even 'jis." If you come from some parts of the East, you may have trouble with "th-" words—"the" becomes "duh," "them" becomes "dem," and so on.

Probably you know your particular weakness already. If not, your instructor, assuming you have one, will call it to your attention, discreetly of course. When this occurs, work hard at eliminating the problem rapidly. If you need extra help, request some appropriate exercises. The sooner you can set aside these minor flaws, the more you will profit from your practice speeches. The latter portion of a speech course is for things more significant than reminders about habitual mispronunciation of ordinary words.

When it comes to the so-called three-dollar words, however, don't expect to outgrow your need for a good dictionary, no matter how many speech courses you take. The very best speakers and scholars accept the use of a dictionary as a fact of life. They are neither too proud nor too busy to call for this assistance. Why should you be?

Oddly enough, getting the correct pronunciation of a difficult word often begins with consciously recognizing that one is not sure of it. People have a tendency, particularly with a word they have seen several times, to think they know the correct sound when really they don't at all. Can you bring to mind any examples? If not, just for beginners, how about the following:

IMPIOUS	SCION
SCHISM	ANALOGOUS
ITALICS	SADISTIC

These words aren't so uncommon that you haven't run across them more than once in something you've read. But if you were called upon to use them tomorrow, perhaps in a quote from someone else, would you know how to pronounce them? Or would you merely think you know, because you had been exposed to them in print once or twice? With words like these, make sure that you haven't been lulled into a dangerous feeling of security.

Before you rise to face an audience, check any words you expect to use in your speech to be certain that you have them right. If you practice your speeches aloud, the verbal deceivers might be discovered more easily but, whatever your method of preparation, don't trust yourself too much. Human nature makes us lazy enough to convince ourselves that there's no reason to investigate a possible stumper.

Even when we know full well that a word needs looking up, we try to slip out of it. By moving on to the next thought we can easily manage to forget the problem entirely. Only by taking some action right on the spot can we catch a fugitive pronunciation before it escapes us once again. That doesn't mean we have to race to the dictionary immediately. If we just write down the word for later action, we have taken a significant step. The problem at least will not be forgotten or set aside so easily.

The next step is determining the pronunciation. Normally this means going to the dictionary—but not always. A dictionary is not likely to contain the name of the fellow from the nearby town who is speaking to your club on pickling cucumbers. If you're going to introduce him, you'll probably have to check with someone who knows him or knows about him. Then, on the day of the speech, a double-check with the person himself is in order. No one named Smythe enjoys being presented as Smith, and the reverse.

From time to time you'll run into other problems in which the ordinary dictionary doesn't help at all—the name of a small town, a school, a road or street, a personality newly arrived in the spotlight. Your ingenuity will come in handy in these instances. When a direct inquiry is impossible, ask your librarian for an appropriate pronunciation guide or for the pronunciation itself. Be aware, also, that the newswire services provide pronunciation lists of new terms or names. Your local radio station or newspaper is likely to have the answer to your problem. Other sources of information are your teachers in the appropriate fields. But don't ask them about words you can easily look up yourself. The one person not to ask is your speech instructor —just before your talk.

With a standard dictionary itself, regardless of which one you use, the necessary procedure is: (1) translate the combination of letters and markings into an actual pronunciation; (2) record that pronunciation in a way that will mean something to you a day or a week later; and (3) gain the ability to say the word correctly at any time without calling attention to it.

The opening pages of your dictionary will tell you how to use its symbols, and usually there are reminders at the bottom of each page. Most dictionaries employ diacritic symbols—markings attached to letters to indicate sounds or emphasis. Think of the several ways of pronouncing the letter "a," for instance, as demonstrated by words such as "care," "father," "tack," and "day." Dictionaries also use special phonetic symbols to represent sounds. The "uh" sound, for example, appears as "ə" whether it represents the "a" of "sofa," the "e" of "over," the first "i" of "affirmation," the "o" of "arbor," the "u" of "focus," or the "y" of martyr." Other phonetic symbols are "ŋ" and "hw." Spend a little time getting acquainted with the symbols and markings your dictionary uses. It can save much time later on.

When it comes to setting down pronunciation for your own reference—which you must do if you expect to retain the correct sound—you may or may not use the same system found in the dictionary. For example, instead of using the "official' method you might create one of your own using syllables and a combination of capital and small letters. "Nation" could be written "NAY-shun," "February" as "FEB-roo-er-ee." The capital letters will help you remember which syllable to stress.

If you use a self-made system, just watch out for syllables that you can't be sure of several days after you write them. It might seem satisfactory to set down "myopic" as "my-OP-ik." But a few days later, would you know if the "O" was long or short? If you wish to use the short "o," a safer way to record the pronunciation might be "my-

OPP-ik." To check your system while you're perfecting it, try your homemade pronunciation keys on a friend. If the friend doesn't get them right, chances are you won't either when the ink is dry. But don't worry. In a short time you'll have the bumps smoothed out.

The last step in fixing a pronunciation lies in using it a few times. Obviously you can't stop a person on a street corner and say, "By the way, did you know that Szeged, on the Yugoslavian border of Hungary, has a population of more than a hundred thousand?" But you can say a word aloud to yourself, alone and in a sentence, instead of just leaving it on paper. And some troublesome words can be used in conversation without making you appear ridiculous.

Whatever you do, take the extra effort that will let you add good *pronunciation* to good *articulation* and good *word selection*. You'll need all three for an effective speech.

EXERCISES

I have not thus far thrust a set of exercises into this book. At this point, however, a few on pronunciation might be useful to you. Considering the tendency to avoid looking up words which we humans have, perhaps the exercises will pull together some of the more common errors and save you from committing them during the next 50 or so years. Do not be dismayed if you find yourself wrong more times than not before checking the answer in a dictionary: The words I've selected are among the ones mispronounced more often than any others.

1. Sometimes we don't put the sounds of a word together with the right emphasis. In the sets of words below circle the ones which indicate the preferred stress in the view of most authorities:

CE-ment	or	ce-MENT
DES-pic-a-ble	or	des-PIC-a-ble
e-LEC-to-ral	or	e-lec-TOR-al
IM-po-tent	or	im-PO-tent
THE-a-tre	or	the-A-tre

2. A few words and names are commonly missed because we confuse them with other words or the sounds in other words. The confusion between the second syllables of February and January is a good example. Using whatever marking system you like, give the preferred pronunciations of the followings words, then in the second column indicate the words with which you think they are often incorrectly associated.

	Preferred Pronunciation	*Incorrect Association*
COLUMN	KAHL-um	volume
HEIGHT		
PENALIZE		
PRONUNCIATION		
SHERBET		
SUITE		
DE GAULLE		
MOSCOW		

3. Another group of trickers are those words that are *not* pronounced as they are spelled. Try these:

ALMOND	
BLACKGUARD	
CHIC	
FLACCID	
OFTEN	
SALMON	

4. Sometimes we do strange things to words. We add sounds to them, we omit sounds, and we turn them around. For the last exercise, have a go at the following. Indicate the preferred pronunciation:

ATHLETE   _____

COUPON   _____

DROWNED   _____

MISCHIEVOUS   _____

DIAMOND   _____

DIAPER   _____

LITERATURE   _____

MATHEMATICS   _____

SOPHOMORE   _____

VICE-VERSA   _____

CAVALRY   _____

ET CETERA   _____

HUNDRED   _____

MODERN   _____

PERSPIRATION   _____

PRESCRIPTION   _____

SPECIAL SPEECHES

chapter 10

Words to Persuade

There is a danger in presenting a separate chapter on persuasion, for it may suggest that it is a speech form unique in its aspects, and that all that has gone before does not apply. Nothing could be farther from truth. Persuasion relies upon almost all the suggestions made in the preceding chapters, and relies upon them heavily. You will succeed or fail depending upon how well the objective is defined in terms of the audience and the moment, how well the speech is organized, how well the attention of the audience is grasped, how well the thesis is made and supported (visually or verbally), how well the speech is delivered. I am saying, simply, that persuasion tests all the powers and abilities of the speaker. It is placed toward the end of the book not because it is so distinct, but because it is so encompassing.

What is persuasion? It is the act of influencing an audience through logical and emotional avenues in order to achieve a particular end. It may comprise the elements of a speech to inform or explain, though its end goes beyond information or instruction. It may be entertaining in parts, but entertainment is not the goal. It may contain words of praise or gratitude, yet courtesy is not the foremost aspect. Persuasion is a way of producing belief, inspiration, conviction and, in one way or another, action.

When do we encounter persuasion? Almost daily in conversational situations, and more frequently than it may first appear in other settings. The pep talk, the sermon, the request for contributions, the business proposal, the speech in behalf of a motion at a club meeting, the anti-war lecture—all are persuasive in nature. In each instance the speaker has a specific goal to which he wishes to lead the audience.

At one end of the persuasive line is the speech to stimulate or inspire, in which a deepening of faith, belief, or feeling is sought; at the other end is the speech to convince, in which agreement or understanding is sought on a possibly controversial issue. In either case, direct or indirect action can and normally should be proposed or implied by the speaker. And appeals to both logic and emotion are proper means of seeking it.

The suggestions for succeeding in persuasion are many, and they have been offered regularly for more than two thousand years. With that kind of precedent, how can I resist offering my own?

THE IDEA

1. *Know clearly the idea you are going to present.* You will need all the clarity and definition required for an informative speech, and then some. Here, according to Plato, is the way Socrates put it:

> Until a man knows the truth of the several particulars of which he is writing or speaking, and is able to define them as they are, and having defined them again to divide them until they can no longer be divided . . . he will be unable to handle arguments . . . either for the purpose of teaching or persuading.[1]

It is necessary, then, for a persuasive speaker to do his homework. As I indicated earlier, that requires the appropriate research (in books or through letters, interviews, or other means), verifying the statistics, checking all quotations.

It may occur to you that statistics, quotations, or other kinds of data, whether you check them or not, are often accepted by audiences.

[1] *Phaedrus*, from the Jowett translation, *The Dialogues of Plato* (Oxford University Press), as reprinted in *Great Books of the Western World* (Chicago: Encyclopaedia Britannica, Inc., 1952), VII, 140. Socrates in this dialogue by Plato also has something to say about speech organization and audience analysis.

Is it worth being fussy about phrases or figures, especially if they will help you just as they stand? Well, I see two reasons to be careful about the items upon which you construct your case. First, if you are building a speech with faulty materials you are building it with straw. It might look good, but the first strong wind will whisk it away. Just as an audience can be led to a false conclusion by unsound arguments, so can you. You might very well present a different and better case with other data before you. Full and accurate information is needed for solid reasoning.

There is a second reason for being clear about all aspects of the idea you are preparing for presentation. The audience may not know you are sketchily prepared, but you will. You simply cannot be as assured in manner with halfway information as you can when you have prepared well. Thus, while the audience may not recognize what is incorrect in what you say, it will hear a speaker not as poised and confident as he might be. Don't underestimate the importance of this general impression in a speech of persuasion. The way the audience reacts to you from the beginning may outweigh anything you say. That may be hard to accept, yet it's a condition of public speaking. It does not, however, justify your thinking only of appearance and not content. Rather, it reinforces the importance of content in building the over-all impression. Confidence comes from having a strong grasp of what you are to present. Confidence is needed if you are to persuade an indifferent or hostile audience. There are other ways of winning the audience, to be sure, and we will examine them. But at the core is knowledge of the idea and its parts.

THE AUDIENCE

2. *Know the audience to which you will present your idea.* Never is audience analysis more important than in the persuasive speech. If the audience is composed of Eskimos to whom you must sell refrigerators it is well to know it in advance.

There are many ways of analyzing audiences. As you become an experienced speaker you probably will devise your own. You might, as Socrates did, classify your listeners in terms of age, temperament, guiding motivations, and value systems, and possibly add education, profession, or area of residence. You might, as Aristotle did, directly relate the categories to probable interests or responses.

"I don't even feel the same way about myself as I did when I was twenty-one. How could I feel the same way about you?"

Reprinted by permission of the artist, John A. Ruge, and the publisher. © 1970 Saturday Review, Inc.

First, though, Aristotle drew profiles of audience types, the best-known being his descriptions of young men, old men, and men in their prime. Here are highlights of Aristotle's analyses, in condensed form. As you read them, think of how you would describe each group—assuming you do not go along with Aristotle's general picture.

Young men have strong passions, and tend to gratify them indiscriminately. Of the bodily desires, it is the sexual by which they are most swayed and in which they show absence of self-control. They are changeable and fickle in their desires, which are violent while they last, but quickly over. . . . Owing to their love of honor they cannot bear being slighted, and are indignant if they imagine themselves unfairly treated. . . .

They look at the good side rather than the bad, not having yet witnessed many instances of wickedness. They trust others readily, because they have not yet often been cheated. . . . Their lives are mainly spent not in memory but in expectation. . . . Their hot tempers and hopeful dispositions make them more courageous than older men are; the hot temper prevents fear, and the hopeful disposition creates confidence. . . .

They have exalted notions, because they have not yet been humbled by life or learnt its necessary limitations; moreover their hopeful disposition makes them think themselves equal to great things. . . . They would always rather do noble deeds than useful ones: their lives are regulated more by moral feeling than by reasoning; and whereas reasoning leads us to choose what is useful, moral goodness leads us to choose what is noble. . . .

All their mistakes are in the direction of doing things excessively and vehemently. . . . They love too much and hate too much. . . . They think they know everything, and are always quite sure about it; this, in fact, is why they overdo everything. . . .

They are ready to pity others, because they think every one an honest man, or anyhow better than he is. . . . They are fond of fun and therefore witty, wit being well-bred insolence.

Having looked at Aristotle's portrait of the young, no doubt with an arched eyebrow, observe what he said about the old:

They have lived many years; they have often been taken in, and often made mistakes; and life on the whole is bad business. The result is that they are sure about nothing and *under-do* everything. They "think," but they never know. . . . They are cynical; that is they tend to put the worst construction on everything. Further, their experience makes them distrustful and therefore suspicious of evil. . . .

They are small-minded, because they have been humbled by life: their desires are set upon nothing more exalted or unusual than what will help to keep them alive. They are not generous, because money is one of the things they must have, and at the same time their experience has taught them how hard it is to get and how easy to lose. They are cowardly, and are always anticipating danger. . . .

They are fond of themselves. . . . Because of this they guide their lives too much by considerations of what is useful and too little by what is noble—for the useful is what is good for oneself, and the noble what is good absolutely. . . .

They lack confidence in the future; partly through experience—for most things go wrong, or anyhow turn out worse than one expects; and partly because of their cowardice. They live by memory rather than by hope; for what is left to them of life is but little as compared with the long past. . . . They are continually talking of the past, because they enjoy remembering it.

Their fits of anger are sudden but feeble. Their sensual passions have either altogether gone or have lost their vigor. . . . Hence men at this time of life are often supposed to have a self-controlled character; the fact is that their passions have slackened. . . .

They guide their lives by reasoning more than by moral feeling; reasoning being directed to utility and moral feeling to moral goodness. . . . Old men may feel pity, as well as young men, but not for the same reason. Young men feel it out of kindness; old men out of weakness, imagining that anything that befalls anyone else might easily happen to them. . . . Hence they are . . . not disposed to jesting or laughter.

If there was an ideal group, to Aristotle's way of thinking, it was men in their prime. They have a character lying between that of the young and that of the old, minus the extremes of either:

To put it generally, all the valuable qualities that youth and age divide between them are united in the prime of life, while all their excesses or defects are replaced by moderation and fitness.[2]

Aristotle went on to consider the type of character produced by fortune or chance: the men of good birth, of wealth, and of power. He also considered their opposites: the unfortunate, the poor, the powerless.

Now, it is not important that you agree with Aristotle in his descriptions of various kinds of human beings, nor is it necessary that you characterize each audience you will face in a descriptive essay. Aristotle's analyses were presented so that you might see the many facets of even a uniform group—old men, young men, and so on. If you will consider each audience—that is, try to know it—you will be more effective. Whether you write a profile or use a checklist is not significant, but studying the audience you seek to persuade is virtually essential if you are to succeed. I hope to show why in the third suggestion for persuasion.

[2] The descriptions from Aristotle's *Rhetoric* are from the translation *The Works of Aristotle* (Oxford University Press), as reprinted in *Great Books,* IX, 636-38.

THE MOTIVATION

3. *Reach the audience and motivate it by the appropriate channel or channels.* Your analysis of the audience is worthless if you don't put it to use. To dwell upon the nobility of a cause in speaking to Aristotle's audience of old men could be as fruitless as urging a dedicated youth group to undertake an activity essentially for financial gain. Remember that you can lead different people or groups to the same end by different means. This doesn't mean being dishonest, either. It simply means utilizing or emphasizing the values which are most important to the group you are addressing.

What are these values? Well, after you get past the basic needs for life, food, for instance, you are confronted by as many groupings of human wants or emotions as there are writers on persuasion. Therefore, an author can't give you a precise or definitive answer. To help you, though, I have set up some channels of motivation which should guide you in preparing a persuasive speech or in preparing a list of your own.

Channels of Motivation

The Moral Channel. This channel is not always easy, for it includes calling up the sense of duty or obligation, something not everyone feels to a significant degree. But with the right audience this channel can be enormously effective. It is one coaches use when they tell their players they must not let the teammates or their tradition down. It is one educators use when they turn parental responsibility into a tax increase for the new school. Salesmen take the same path to turn parental responsibility into encyclopedia purchases. The moral channel brings good response from any group of individuals clearly dedicated to a cause: graduates of military academies or aviation programs, seminarians, Peace Corps volunteers, sincere charity workers, sincere members of religious congregations, advanced science or medical students. Lawyers have found that a moral argument can work well with juries.

You will note that I have not designated this channel as emotional or logical. That is because it, like the others I present, can have parallel currents. If an appeal calls forth an emotion—as in the use of sympathy to obtain funds to combat a disease of children—that does not mean it is not at the same time logical to fight disease. Only fanatics or demagogs set aside logic in making their appeals, and often they take pains to give the illusion of logical reasoning.

Recognize, then, that as we consider ways of reaching audiences in terms of what is important to them, we are assuming that logic will not be divorced from human wants and emotions—nor human wants and emotions from logic. It is the rare individual who reacts to a cold, abstract presentation that touches on nothing human. In Nazi Germany it was this kind of person who followed orders and liquidated "useless" old people or supervised the breeding of human stock to improve the species.

Concentrate upon logic or wants and emotions as the moment demands, but don't feel that you must separate them and deliver an academically pure speech. Instead, try to blend them, even as the insurance salesman does. First he touches on fear and pity while appealing to the sense of responsibility of the prospective client: "What would happen to your family if you should, God forbid, . . . ?" Then, he shows the practical side of investing in insurance, the instant estate, the enforced savings program, the retirement benefits—all the while mentioning the peace of mind the individual will enjoy because of his investment. When it appears that the customer is convinced of the need for insurance, the agent stresses the advantage of his company or service, perhaps showing the logic of a particular plan. At last he introduces the action step and gets the client to sign an application (with no obligation) before increased age puts him into a higher fee bracket and means greater danger of failing the physical examination: "Who knows what tomorrow will bring?" Considering the amount of insurance sold in this country each year, the agent's technique of blending emotional and logical currents has to be considered a good example of persuasion, or at least an effective one.

The Vital Channel. Here is the channel closest to the basic needs of the human being. It concerns his desire to stay alive and, to a lesser degree, to stay well. Staying alive means having sleep, food, air, water, and, in most situations, protection from the elements—through clothing and shelter—and protection from danger. Staying well means having the right food, some exercise, proper medical care and, in today's hectic world, a bit of inner calm.

When you as a speaker approach an audience by the vital channel, you are appealing to instincts of self or group preservation. If you can relate a subject to that instinct and make the audience see the relationship, you are well on your way to winning your case, especially if a particular need or fear is strong in your listeners' minds at the moment. On the other hand, a vital appeal can be weak, if the problem or fear of it seems remote. Food or space problems thirty years from now don't bother people as much as five-minute delays in ticket lines today. The anti-smoking campaigns have been as thorough and logical as they could reasonably be expected to be, yet they have had little impact on people who think it won't happen to them or can't be worried about diseases that seem a long way off. But give a vital problem the fearful imminency of the Black Plague in the 1300s or of the Persians knocking at the gates, and the audience responds readily. In a comfortable society, expect to use the vital channel in conjunction with some other, unless you can generate enough anger or apprehension in your listeners to make them react. Complacency is not easily overcome.

The Physical Channel. This path to persuasion is closely related to the vital channel, but does not involve basic needs for life. The speaker using this pathway speaks of a listener's desire for comfort, physical recreation, rest, and the like. It is a favorite channel of the television advertiser, who offers his product so that the viewer might be cooler in summer, cozy in winter, fresh all day, free from itching, full of vigor, and not thirsty after the second beer.

Oddly, appeals to physical pleasure are often easier than those involving more serious needs. Immediacy has to be a factor which enhances the effect of this channel, otherwise air conditioners would sell better in winter. But winter or summer, there are things which please people physically. To ask people to join a ski club without emphasizing the many physical pleasures associated with the activity would seem foolish. Included among the "physical pleasures" are those of the senses: taste, smell, feeling, and even seeing and hearing. Laughing, then, is a physical pleasure as, of course, is lovemaking or walking barefoot in the sand.

If you are not certain how to employ the physical channel in persuasion, simply pick up a popular magazine or turn on the television set and see what the advertisers are doing. You will learn more than you could from any textbook—even this one.

The Intellectual Channel. Perhaps we should have considered this path before getting lost in physical pleasure. Be that as it may, the mind is a wondrous agency and should not be overlooked as something to appeal to directly. Oh, you won't very often have someone say, "The brilliance and coherence of your argument are so great that I will support your position for that reason alone." Nevertheless, you can advance your case through intellectual means. And by this we don't mean only the obvious path of reason and logic.

As you may have observed in watching young children, there is delight in learning, even in learning for its own sake. Incredible as it may seem to teachers on bad days, that delight does not entirely vanish as we grow older. People still like to learn, given the right circumstances. Therefore, if you stimulate them intellectually by a bit of informal instruction in your persuasive speech, you might be making them more receptive to your ultimate message. In some instances the education itself is enough to let you win your case. But sneak the teaching in carefully. You don't wish to offend or scare off your pupils.

The desire to learn is related closely to curiosity. If you can bring forth that natural instinct, you can keep the audience with you in many situations where you might otherwise lose it. The old burlesque pitchmen worked so heavily on creating mystery about the items they were selling between acts that they were able to get a half-dollar for gadgets, booklets, and candy not worth ten cents. I don't recommend that kind of career, but I do suggest you utilize curiosity in leading listeners to your main points. Here is another technique you can study by opening a magazine or watching television. The ads which catch your eye but don't immediately give away the basic message are the ones I refer to. Curiosity, of course, is normally a pathway to some other appeal, but it can be used alone with certain subjects: those in which you are saying, "Wouldn't you like to know . . . ?" or "How would you like to see . . . ?"

Earlier in this book we looked at the use of wit in a speech. It too is a way of reaching listeners through intellectual means. An audience that appreciates your wit will at least listen to your message. The correct application of natural humor to the situation at hand can both relieve tension and show that you are a thinking person. Remember the suggestions and cautions about using it, however. And don't use humor just to show off. As Adlai Stevenson put it on the RCA album cover for "The Wit of JFK":

> Laughter is shared by equals. It cannot be bestowed with condescension.

The Acquisitional Channel. It has often been said that ours is a materialistic society. If that is so, the speaker cannot close his eyes to it whether he likes that fact or not. Actually, for as long as we have records man has been busy acquiring or saving things. The nature of what he has sought or put away has varied somewhat through the centuries—and from society to society—but you can be sure that until you are through making speeches your audiences will comprise people with acquisitional interests of some kind.

Some people are concerned with the more material acquisitions: property, money, dancing girls. Others strive for things of the spirit or intellect: a deeper faith, a good education, a reserved seat inside the Pearly Gates. The groups are not mutually exclusive, though. The man of property might be a true humanitarian; the man of education might be an unrestrained collector of books. Both probably will have great interest in gaining time with which to pursue their interests. Either might wish to acquire more energy for his tasks or hair for his head.

Butcher, banker, or baker, everyone wishes to obtain or preserve something. If you know what that something is for a particular audience, show how to acquire it and you won't have to worry too much about other channels of motivation.

The Interpersonal Channel. There is a hard-to-define area of human interest which has to do with our relationships with other people. Except for hermits and others who have withdrawn from the world, human beings to some extent relate their happiness or lack of it to the way their lives intertwine with those of others. Analysts of our interpersonal relationships write about group approval, the competitive urge, reputation, leadership, cooperation, pride, imitation, and the like. In varying degrees, these things are important to individuals. As a persuasive speaker you must take them into consideration.

Some people like to be leaders. In your proposal, can you offer them a way to exert leadership? Some people, particularly the young, have public idols they admire. Can you enhance your message by identifying it with a personality they might emulate or imitate? Some people like to stay a step ahead of their friends and neighbors. Will your message show them how to do so? Some people are highly concerned about what people think of them. Will your proposal, without any sacrifice to principle, offer them reassurance?

As you can see, the interpersonal-relationships channel may be used to attain an end that could hold no interest for an audience member were he alone on this planet. The matter is not of life or death, but one of belonging, leading, sharing, following. These are the feelings to keep in mind when the interpersonal-relationships channel is your path to persuasion.

We have considered six channels for motivating audiences. They are neither a magic six nor an absolute six. If you would like to revise, enlarge, or combine them, do so by all means. It will show that you have been thinking enough about persuasion to have ideas of your own. And in the long run it will be your ideas that will carry you. These, however, should serve well enough till you are ready to go out on your own.

Why were emotions—sympathy, fear, anger—referred to within other headings? Because they normally underlie or support the various motivational channels. While it may be wise to condition an audience for the central message by building upon or developing feelings of anger or fear, calmness or confidence, seldom does an emotion become the primary channel or the desired end of persuasion. Further, the different emotions may be so intermixed in a situation or presentation that it would be difficult to decide exactly which emotional chord is dominant.

In most circumstances you will handle emotions within or in advance of the principal argument. Obviously, you would not press a serious recommendation upon an agitated and hostile audience without first trying to bring it to a state of calm. At the same time you would expect to light a little fire under an indifferent group. Be aware of the importance of emotions and integrate them with your presentation, but don't play upon them. That is the technique of dictators, rabble-rousers, lynch mobs. Yes, emotional overtones are heavy in some speeches—the pep talk in the locker room, for example—yet there usually is a logical and moral aspect to such talks which keeps the intended outcome above the level of mere frenzy. Yes, lawyers have saved lives with emotional closing appeals, yet these addresses follow carefully laid-out cases which normally are reviewed in the summation. What is more, to the defendant, the situation is something of an emergency!

Seek or employ an emotional response in persuasion if you will, but use it honestly and not irrelevantly. It isn't very difficult to take away something from a friend by deceit; it isn't anything to be proud of either. And when the truth comes out, you have lost a friend. I'll have more to say about fair play in the fourth general suggestion for persuasion.

THE ARGUMENT

4. *Present the argument intelligently and fairly.* No one, of course, sets forth to present an unsound, muddled argument. A great number of them come out that way, however. I sincerely hope that what you may have learned from this book, coupled with your own good sense and experience, will keep your arguments intelligent and well organized. The challenge of persuasion requires your best efforts.

As you review your presentation prior to delivery, regard it for a moment not as something you yourself will be saying but as an argument that might come from another. Give it every test you would expect to give another person's attempt to persuade you. If you find a flaw in your chain of reasoning, try to correct it. If it remains a point easily refuted, get it out of your speech before it reaches the audience. If it is faulty reasoning that nevertheless might slip by, your obligation still is to remove it.

What does it matter if a fallacious argument is presented and no one notices? Let's hear what Socrates had to say about that in talking with a young man named Phaedrus:

SOCRATES: Suppose that I persuaded you to buy a horse and go to the wars. Neither of us knew what a horse was like, but I knew that you believed a horse to be of [the] tame animals the one that has the longest ears.

PHAEDRUS: That would be ridiculous.

SOCRATES: There is something more ridiculous coming. Suppose, further, that I . . . composed a speech in honor of an ass, whom I entitled a horse, beginning: "A noble animal and a most useful possession, especially in war . . . you may get on his back and fight, and he will carry baggage or anything."

PHAEDRUS: How ridiculous!

SOCRATES: Yes; but is not even a ridiculous friend better than a cunning enemy?

PHAEDRUS: Certainly.

SOCRATES: And when the orator instead of [merely] putting an ass in place of a horse, puts good for evil, being himself ignorant of their true nature . . . and hav-

> ing studied the notions of the multitude, falsely
> persuades . . . not about "the shadow of an ass,"
> which he confuses with a horse, but about the good
> which he doesn't recognize as evil, what will be
> the harvest . . . ?
>
> PHAEDRUS: The reverse of good.[3]

I hope, then, that if in your preparation you discover that the long-eared animal in your argument is not really a horse, you will not go ahead and ride it anyway.

What are the dangers in argument to watch for? Many of them I have already mentioned, but it wouldn't hurt to draw them and other threats to sound and honest persuasion into capsule form.

Errors in Reasoning

A. *Cut-rate induction:* reasoning from the particular to the general on the basis of insufficient or invalid sampling. Remember the story of the blind men deciding what the elephant was on the basis of the individual parts each one touched?

B. *Sloppy deduction:* attempting to apply formal deductive logic to a situation without also applying the necessary rules and safeguards. Careless reasoners can come up with this kind of syllogism:

> *All giraffes have long necks.*
> *Harvey has a long neck.*
> *Therefore, Harvey is a giraffe.*

The beginning generalization seems safe enough. Men have seen enough giraffes to induce that all giraffes have long necks. The second statement, about Harvey's neck, can be taken at face value. But this particular, together with the beginning general statement, does not lead to a correct deduction that Harvey is a giraffe—or a communist. It is nonetheless the kind of deduction that appears all the time. Many alternatives have to be ruled out before Harvey's long neck makes him a giraffe. Sloppy deduction ignores the alternatives, while also forming tangled syllogisms.

C. *Unproved causation:* putting together two things in a cause-and-effect relationship when none exists. One event can follow another

---

[3] *Phaedrus, Great Books,* VII, 131, with slight amendment.

without the first event necessarily being the cause of the second. Further, any cause can have more than one effect, and any effect more than one cause. A pure cause-and-effect relationship can occur only if the supposed cause is the only one possible and is sufficient to bring about the effect. Is the starter's gun the cause of a race?

Flaws in Presentation

A. *Lack of clarity:* leaving key terms undefined; confusing the audience by using a single word to mean more than one thing; speaking in jargon to an audience of nonspecialists.

B. *Faulty analogy:* supporting a point with a comparison in which the things compared are not sufficiently alike in all pertinent aspects.

C. *Inaccuracy:* using incorrect quotations, questionable statistics, out-of-date information, unverified data. Of all the material used incorrectly, statistics must stand at or near the top of the list. A day before writing this paragraph I heard a naturalist tell an audience that his vocation was the country's leading outdoor avocation or recreation. How did he know? Because in the preceding year 150,000,000 people had entered national parks—more than had gone to baseball or football stadiums, golf courses, and so forth.

Now, this gentleman was sincere in his use of this statistic, but let's look at it. We should, because, as he used it, it means that three out of four Americans went to national parks that year. What was the source of his information? The naturalist didn't say, but it must have been a combined head count of some sort. If so, how would anyone know whether 150,000,000 different people visited national parks or whether each of 50,000,000 people entered three parks? The head count would be the same—and certainly families often visit several parks on the same trip. Further, we could wonder if the figure included the national historical, military, and battlefield parks, which would attract people for reasons not connected with nature. In other words, a startling statement was supported by a vague statistic from sources unknown. This listener, for one, needed more to be convinced.

Deceits in Presentation

A. *Calling names:* using emotion-laden, negative words to damage the image of persons, institutions, nations, ideas. The same individual might be described by a friend as calm and patient in manner, by an enemy as cold and indifferent. Avoid wallowing in emotionally negative words.

B. *Arguing ad hominem:* directing the argument not to the issues but against men associated with them. If enough dislike can be generated against an individual, for example, the cause for which he stands good or bad, also suffers. The late Senator Joseph McCarthy, in a famous speech in West Virginia in 1950, mixed name calling with an argument *ad hominem* in describing the Secretary of State in this manner:

> . . . As you know, very recently the Secretary of State proclaimed his loyalty to a man guilty of what has always been considered as the most abominable of all crimes—of being a traitor to the people who gave him a position of great trust. The Secretary of State in attempting to justify his continued devotion to the man who sold out the Christian world to the atheistic world, referred to Christ's Sermon on the Mount as justification and reason therefor, and the reaction of the American people would have made the heart of Abraham Lincoln happy.
>
> When this pompous diplomat in striped pants, with a phony British accent, proclaimed to the American people that Christ on the Mount endorsed communism, high treason, and betrayal of a sacred trust, the blasphemy was so great that it awakened the dormant indignation of the American people. . . .[4]

I am sure you can recognize the hostile words, "striped pants" included, as well as the argument *ad hominem* without any underlining by me. Keep the preceding quotation in mind, though. I will come back to it.

C. *Exploiting hates and fears:* opposing an issue or ticket or program by relating it to a dreaded or hated object. The ever-present communist "plot" has to be the best current example of this device. The McCarthy speech from which our quotation was taken was based entirely on the menace of communism, which, in the speaker's mind, was fast taking over the government.

D. *Forming two camps:* narrowing the many aspects of a prob-

---

[4] *Major Speeches and Debates of Senator Joe McCarthy Delivered in the United States Senate 1950-1951* (Washington, D.C.: Government Printing Office, 1952), p. 14.

lem to an imagined us-them, either-or relationship. Can this planet be divided simply into "the Christian world and the atheistic world"? Are things so uncomplicated that people are either rich or poor, enlightened or unenlightened, have's or have-not's?

E. *Misdirecting thinking:* distracting the audience from the main issue by throwing in a minor, possibly irrelevant, but often dramatic one. This deceit employs the so-called "red herring," the action or object on which hatred, fear, or praise can be focused while the main one is conveniently overlooked. The dictator Mussolini received abundant plaudits around the world for making the trains of Italy run on time. But after a time even the efficiency of his dictatorship could not keep people from noticing the more serious problems in his nation.

F. *Using improper testimonials:* employing untrustworthy or biased authorities, false or distorted quotations, and statements out of context to win approval for an argument. People often say "If it's good enough for Doctor X it's good enough for me!" The question then is: is it really good enough for Doctor X? And is Doctor X unprejudiced in his thinking? And how long ago, and under what circumstances, did he make his statement?

G. *Creating questionable associations:* allying a cause with a respected individual or institution when no such association is indicated. To do so is to gain prestige or support that is undeserved. Was a witch-hunting reaction by the American people really something that "would have made the heart of Abraham Lincoln happy"?

H. *Putting two issues into one:* operating on an "if . . . then" principle without acknowledging the "if." The user of this device doesn't bother proving guilt, he advocates punishment on the assumption that the party is guilty: "If we are ever going to get our industry back to its former level of prosperity we will have to rid it of the scourge of unionism!" You must be certain one issue is established before whacking away at another.

I. *Setting up strawmen:* posing arguments or statements that are not exactly those of an opponent and then deftly demolishing them. "Spurgeon Smedley would have us believe that the blood pressure of every American would improve if bromide were put in our water systems. Well, let me say. . . ." Poor Smedley may never have thought that at all, yet he winds up being shot down for something he never proposed.

Dwelling longer on these dangers might make you think I don't trust you. I do. Please take this section as a guide to judging an argument as well as to presenting one. I regret that you will encounter many of the deceits in presentation as you go through life. I regret equally that these tricks of persuasion do work quite frequently—and some speech books propose using a few of them. All I can say in return is that the speaker who is ethical, who uses logic aided by but not smothered in emotion, will in the long run do better than the trickster who wins battles but, when his reputation becomes known, loses wars.

To people who know you, you cannot divorce what you say from what you are. No quick trick can give you back integrity once you have lost it. You will not always speak to fools or to those easily taken in by half-truths or loaded words. Sooner or later you have to rely upon logical, motivated argument or lose the day. In this context, then, it is wiser to be invited through the front door than to slip in the bedroom window. The latter may be more effective, depending upon your objective, but one day that window will be locked. And once a person has been caught hanging on the windowsill it is too late to use the front door.

But all this is stating things negatively. Ours is a basically honest society. Despite our fussing, we file our income tax returns truthfully, behave fairly well when no one's looking, tell the truth when it counts. Should not our speeches be at least as honest as our society? It is one thing to win; it is another to know you have won the right way. There are more than enough right ways to win in speech without having to bother about the dishonest ones.

And now a last suggestion for persuasion:

THE PATTERN

5. *Use an organizational pattern appropriate to the audience's perception of the issue.* Just as you must meet your hearers at their emotional level, calming or arousing them as necessary, you must also meet them at their point of knowledge and analysis. In fact, that may be the only way to put sparks into them, for unknown problems aren't much to get excited about.

Any of the patterns mentioned in Chapter Four can be used, possibly in combination, in the persuasive speech. In the speech to convince, however, the logical patterns dominate. One, cause-and-effect, has been described in detail. The *problem-solution pattern* has been put off till now. With any subject in controversy it is a strong approach.

Speeches to convince are made because of problems. If there is no problem to resolve, no controversy, persuasion takes the form of stimulation or inspiration by which audiences are led to feel more, to believe more, and possibly to do more. Such audiences often have to be put in motion, but not convinced—except to get up and move. Convincing involves:

1. A problem: something to resolve.
2. Controversy: several ways to resolve it.
3. Recommendation: the speaker's way of resolving it, based upon his analysis.
4. Actuation: the setting in motion of the recommended resolution or related suggestion.

Now, an audience you hope to convince may, as a whole, have any degree of conviction. The problem could be brand new, not even heard of by most present. Or it might be something that just has come to light, so that there has been no time as yet to really think of solutions. On the other hand, a controversy may have been raging for some time and many of the listeners may have a strong idea about how to handle it. They may indeed be on the verge of action. Their analysis and plan of action may or may not be yours.

Begin, then, where you expect to find most of the audience. If necessary, educate them on the subject in question. It is pointless to go on without doing so—and a well-reasoned, honest piece of instruction will help greatly when it comes to acting on a recommendation. Even when the problem is not unknown, a concise review is helpful, if only to let people know that you see the issue fully and fairly. When the audience knows both the problem and the available courses of action at the outset, you should still review it briefly but soundly, then explore the several paths to resolution. It is unwise to say only negative or belittling things about an approach with which you disagree, for you will offend those who at that point believe in it. If you give their plan some respect, they are much more likely to listen to yours. Remember, it is better to be thought of as one interested in solving a problem than as one simply advocating a particular plan. The audience must reason along with you if it is to be pulled to your proposal. Try to have the listeners saying to themselves as you go along: "Yes, that's right. That's right."

Normally the last viewpoint you introduce is the one you favor. On it you will expand, combining your logic with the motivations of your listeners. When you are finished, you desire more than a "That's nice" from the audience. You hope that your argument will have been so compelling that your listeners have no choice but to go along with you—not for emotional reasons, but because reason and logic and their own motivations make your way the only sensible one. Ben Franklin reflected this approach in a speech he prepared in behalf of the adoption of the Constitution. He showed why he was compelled to sign it by the very line of reasoning he offered to others. In part, Franklin stated:

> . . . Mr. President, I agree to this Constitution, with all its faults—if they are such—because I think a general government [is] necessary for us, and there is no form of government but what may be a blessing to the people if well administered. . . . I doubt too whether any other convention we can obtain may be able to make a better Constitution; for when you assemble a number of men, to have the advantage of their joint wisdom, you inevitably assemble with those men, all their prejudices, their passions, their errors of opinion, their local interests, and selfish views. From such an assembly can a perfect production be expected?

Franklin was saying that the new country's leaders could sign what could very well be a fine constitution, and get on with the business of government, or they could delay and try again, and possibly not come up with a document as good.

No doubt thinking of how his Albany Plan of Union had failed to get enough support in colonial legislatures after the Albany Congress passed it in 1754, Franklin gave reason not merely for approval, but strong approval:

> [I]t . . . astonishes me, sir, to find this system approaching so near perfection as it does; and I think it will astonish our enemies, who are waiting with confidence to hear that our counsels are confounded like those of the builders of Babel, and that our States are on point of separation, only to meet hereafter for the purpose of cutting one another's throats. . . . Much of the strength and efficiency of any government in procuring and securing happiness to the people depends on opinion, on the general opinion, of the goodness of that gov-

ernment, as well as the wisdom and integrity of its governors. I hope therefore, for our own sake, as a part of the people, and for the sake of our posterity, that we shall act heartily and unanimously in recommending this Constitution, wherever our influence may extend. . . . I cannot help expressing a wish that every member of the convention who may still have objections to it would with me on this occasion doubt a little of his own infallibility, and, to make manifest our unanimity, put his name to this instrument.[5]

Ben Franklin, wise man that he was, did not wish to leave things with his associates merely agreeing with him; therefore he gave them strong and somewhat urgent reasons for them to put their names to the instrument. It is intelligent to provide listeners with a path to follow, especially if you have won them to your side. Sometimes the path is obvious—signing, voting, donating. Still, in planning any speech to convince—or to inspire, for that matter—be sure to ask yourself: "How do I wish to leave the audience?" While those in it may have no opportunity to vote or sign or give, there are still things you might wish them to do other than applaud politely when you are finished. People can write their Congressman, send for more information on your proposal, accept and examine an application blank for the club, give you their names and phone numbers, and so on. Don't leave it to them to work things out, though: Provide the Congressman's address or any other information they need, and possibly paper and pen, too.

Even if you sense that the audience remains unconvinced, you need not omit the actuation phase. If your presentation was well ordered and well delivered you may have caused your hearers to accept the possibility that your ideas have merit. They might read the literature you ask them to look at, or watch an upcoming television program on the issue, or come to another meeting. Recognize that getting a person whose position is opposite yours to move a little in your direction is as much an achievement as moving a neutral party a step off dead center. Very often you or one of your supporters will have another crack at that fellow you nudged a bit. That may in fact be in your plan—and is one more good reason not to try those questionable devices of persuasion. They may have worn off by the second speech.

[5] Benjamin Franklin, "On Signing the Constitution," in Aly, *American Short Speeches,* pp. 16-18.

In review, then, here are our five general suggestions for persuasion:

1. Know clearly the idea you are going to present.
2. Know the audience to which you will present it.
3. Reach the audience and motivate it by the appropriate channel or channels.
4. Present the argument intelligently and fairly.
5. Use an organizational pattern appropriate to the audience's perception of the issue.

chapter 11

Words of Praise and Gratitude

It is impossible to predict the kinds of speeches you will make in your lifetime. The chances are good, however, that you will make one of those covered in this chapter. Perhaps not the eulogy, but quite possibly one of the other speeches of courtesy—the introduction, the award presentation, or the tribute. As an educated person your world will be one in which guest speakers must be introduced, awards for service or accomplishment must be presented, "thank you's" must be said. I hope that the suggestions offered in the next few pages will help you with these special occasions.

THE SPEECH OF INTRODUCTION

Let us begin with the most common courtesy speech, that of introduction. Normally it is of a speaker, yet it can be of a film or other presentation. The basic requirement, nevertheless, remains to prepare a smooth path for what is to follow, be it live or recorded.

Your first task as an introducer may be to settle the audience. If the program begins with your remarks, the members of the audi-

"Now we owe them a dinner."

ence probably will be engaged in dozens of small conversations. Their
attention must be switched from the many separate topics and focused
on the main one at hand. Recognize this requirement, use the suggestions for beginning offered in Chapter Three, and take satisfaction in
delivering to the next speaker a more attentive audience than you received. You will have earned your money if you do nothing else.

Yet there is more you can do. After capturing the attention of
your listeners, you can whet their appetites. Without delivering the
next speaker's talk, or offering a scene-by-scene preview of a film,
make those present eager to witness the main event—which isn't you,
remember. I have seen introductory speakers become so carried away
at being in the spotlight that they consumed time which belonged to
the person they were assigned to present, all the while boring the
audience to desperation.

One way to create interest in the person you are introducing is
to show that he is qualified to speak on the subject. People like to

hear experts, even minor ones. Avoid smothering your listeners with information, but tell them enough about your successor to make them respect him. Select those aspects you would like to know about were you in the audience.

You may have to discover the items yourself, for not always does biographical data precede the speaker. When it doesn't, write for it. If time doesn't permit writing and phone connections are impossible, get as much information as you can in the minutes before the program and don't try for anything but a brief speech. You can have some statements planned in advance—about the subject or occasion, perhaps —then fit the last-minute biographical data to it. At least do one very important thing: Obtain the correct pronunciation of the speaker's name.

If there is a timeliness about the occasion, be sure to mention it. You rarely will have the good fortune to be introducing a direct descendant of Christopher Columbus on October 12th, but you may have an income tax specialist on April 7th or a respected gardener in the first week of spring. Even a nonexpert can appear more interesting if he faces an audience at an appropriate time. Always look for this relationship, though it may not be apparent at first glance.

It is not a bad idea, when preparing an introductory speech, to put yourself for the moment in the place of the person being introduced. Why? Because it may suggest some things you should not say. Always remember the individuality of audiences, which we have considered several times. Your guest will be aware of it and could be embarrassed by a statement inappropriate for a particular group. As an extreme example, a Congressman would not relish being introduced to a group of industrialists as organized labor's best friend in Washington. Under few circumstances would he enjoy having you indicate that the woman sitting beside him at the head table is his fourth wife. He may or may not appreciate being referred to familiarly by his first name, especially if you met him only moments before. It's dismaying, the frequency with which things like these happen in speeches of introduction.

Possibly the worst thing you can do, oddly enough, is to be too nice. Overpraise is a heavy burden to carry. The audience is made to expect too much. The speaker, unless he thinks himself divine, feels the extra pressure of being called the wisest, the bravest, the most eloquent, the wittiest person ever to take the platform. By telling an audience to "get ready to laugh as they never laughed before," you virtually assure your successor an array of faces locked into make-me-laugh expressions.

How long should your introduction be? No longer than necessary to accomplish the several things I have mentioned. When the audience is quiet, receptive, and aware of the speaker's background, it is time for you to sit down. In some instances the speaker is so well known, or of such stature or position, that his introduction is a formality:

> Ladies and gentlemen, the President of the United States.

Rarely are the requirements of introduction so substantial that more than three minutes are needed to handle them. Former Chancellor of the University of Southern California, Rufus B. Von KleinSmid used only one minute in making this extemporaneous introduction of Joseph Francis Cardinal McIntyre:

> I am particularly privileged tonight to listen to his eminence Cardinal McIntyre. Born in the city of New York, he early dedicated himself to the church. But the necessities of the situation required that he go to work. And so he entered the service of Wall Street and rose very rapidly until, at the age of 28, he was offered a partnership in the firm which he had served first as an errand boy. Instead, he entered the priesthood, which, as everybody in this room attests, was our great good fortune.
>
> I present him to you with great personal pleasure.[1]

THE SPEECH OF PRESENTATION

It could be said that this speech is the one in which old George is given the gold watch after 50 years of loyal service, but that would be making light of a meaningful occasion. Life is studded with situations in which people give other people tangible or symbolic evidences of their esteem or admiration. It may be for long service, as with George, or for specific achievement, as in the football lineman-of-the-year award. Or it may be because a well-liked person is at a turning point in life—quitting a job to get married or moving to another city. Whether the gift is a china teapot or a neatly inscribed certificate, the award doesn't mean much if the recipient merely re-

[1] As transcribed from the broadcast of the Baccalaureate service of the University of Southern California, CBS Radio Pacific Network, June 16, 1957.

ceives it in the mail. A presentation ceremony, even a brief and informal one, is the customary and nicer way of doing things.

If you are the presenter, you speak not for yourself alone but for those gathered there to do honor. You cannot, of course, say everything that all those attending would wish you to say—nor should you worry about pleasing everybody, an impossibility. You can, however, accomplish the basic assignment in more than satisfactory manner if you:

1. Tell who is giving the award or gift, if it is not self-evident.
2. Tell what the award or gift stands for, be it a simple token of friendship or a trophy recognizing achievement of precise requirements.
3. Tell why the recipient was selected.
4. Offer an appropriate closing to your speech, possibly using challenge or quotation.

And don't forget to give the recipient his award should that be included in your duties.

Sometimes the identity of the awardee is a secret till the moment of presentation, so your last line may be drowned by applause if not designed correctly. Naturally, when there is a secret winner, you will wish to build the suspense as you proceed. Beware, then, of spoiling things by a too-specific reference to Mr. X early in your remarks. Say that the fellow could react quickly on the playing field; don't say he was the team's starting quarterback, a sure giveaway.

Closely related to the speech of presentation is the *speech of welcome*. No gift is made—save, perhaps, for the keys to the city—but the speaker, on behalf of others, extends a greeting to the new resident or honored visitor. He tells for whom he speaks, expresses hospitality, and says a few kind words about the newcomer or guest. He must in a few moments generate a feeling of warmth that can begin making friends of strangers. Without boasting about his group or overpraising the newcomer, he must let each side see some of the good points of the other, spiritual as well as material. "The door is open; we're delighted to have you here" is his theme.

THE SPEECH OF RESPONSE

Following the presentation of an award, a welcome, or a speech of tribute, there often is a short response from the person honored.

If you are fortunate enough to be in this situation but so surprised that you have prepared no speech, remember that all you will be saying is "Thank you." People will accept exactly those words—but they will be a little disappointed if you don't say a little more. "Speech! Speech!" is what you are likely to hear.

What can you say beyond the "Thank you"? That you are honored or pleased by the generosity and kindness expressed. Why? Because you have always held the group in fond esteem; you were selected from among a group of fine competitors or teammates several of whom were as deserving of the award as you; you have always hoped that someday this honor would be yours.

If the award was for specific accomplishment, there may be someone to whom you are grateful for advice or instruction. Mention his or her contribution, in brief but specific terms. "I want to thank my director . . ." is heard often on television or movie awards programs. The practice has been so overdone that it doesn't mean much unless the speaker tells how the assistance was so important. If it wasn't, why, except for flattery, should it be singled out?

Often the winning of an award or honor is a symbol of a culmination of learning and accomplishment of far greater significance than the award itself. For the benefit of those who will follow you, you might share the meaningful aspects of the steps along the line—the lesson learned by painful experience, the quiet boost from someone years before, the satisfaction that comes from at last putting together all the pieces of learning and experience in efficient manner. Such remarks can lend both a human and an inspirational touch to your response.

Inspiration can also be found in your expression of what the honor means and will mean to you. Will it serve as a reminder of your obligation to continue to meet its standards? Will it, if you are passing to a new phase of life, be a reminder of an important and rewarding period of your education or career? Try to thank the donors not only for what their gift or honor is, but for what it will be.

THE SPEECH OF TRIBUTE

Akin to the speeches of presentation and welcome, but not quite the same, are the speeches of tribute. Usually they are delivered at unique events—or on special anniversaries—and the person or persons honored may or may not be present. A testimonial dinner is such an occasion, but more frequently encountered is a dedication of a monument or a funeral service.

I separate the *testimonial* affair from an awards ceremony, although it may include an award, because it normally reflects not a specific accomplishment or visit but an accumulation of admiration and respect. So close to the memorial or burial service is it, in fact, that recipients of the testimonial tribute have been heard to remark in humorous fashion, "Everyone was so nice in what they said I thought I was at my own funeral." More than one tough baseball player has been known to shed tears when, toward the end of his career, the fans gathered at the stadium for his night.

In paying tribute to a living individual, the speaker tries to express what that person has meant to the group assembled, to the community or nation, to his profession. Here is the tribute motion picture leader Charles Brackett paid to director George Cukor at a special dinner in his honor:

> George Cukor is responsible for bringing me to Hollywood. This misdates us thoroughly, making me sound like a sprout he'd discovered and in whom he saw promise. Before your guest of honor blows a gasket, let it be thoroughly understood that at that moment he was just a kid turning to a mature writer for some work on a script. Indeed, later, he so turned to Mr. Somerset Maugham. [Laughter] Anyway, I proved completely inadequate for the picture I was supposed to work on and left town at the expiration of my contract with only one big gain, George Cukor's friendship. It has enriched me ever since.
>
> I have only had the privilege of working with him once on a picture since that long-ago first effort. You have to work with a great many other directors to appreciate that privilege. Then you know the beautiful ring in Cukor's voice when, disputing some question of casting or set construction or some story point, he speaks up in protest: "We can't do it, it's phoney, phoney, phoney, *phoney!*" I don't know whether that is more condemnatory than when he merely says "That's phoney!" In fact, Dick Breen, Walter Reisch and I used to count the number of "phonies" in his pronouncements—the timing and the emphasis on them—both for our guidance and our delight.
>
> To sound a more serious note, let me focus on what to me is his most important contribution to the art of the cinema—and

don't think I am going to single out any of the great motion pictures he has made. It's something more impersonal, it's the standard he raised. I've never seen an adequate essay comparing great acting on the stage and great acting in motion pictures. Having been an addict of the theatre all my life, it was years before I discovered that I don't much like stage acting anymore, even at its best. I find it inferior to motion picture acting at its best. On the stage the effort shows, the actors have to project too hard. Every gesture has to be a little exaggerated, every facial expression has to get a little out of drawing. To an eye trained to the understatement of great picture acting the effect is false. The reason I bring it up tonight is that I think your guest of honor, George Cukor, is more responsible for that difference than any one person. It's that inner ear of his, whispering, "That's phoney!" and eliminating the falsity in the performance he's dealing with, which set the standard. Other great directors have achieved the standard, of course, but I think of George as a kind of pitchpipe—no wonder it's easy to assemble a great cast when the actors and actresses learn Cukor is to be the director. He can get undreamed-of values out of any of them; they should pay for the chance to work with him.

Ladies and gentlemen, tonight you have the rare privilege of honoring a great man and a man without a pretentious bone in his body. Correction, that isn't a rare privilege—it's unique.[2]

Mr. Brackett, as you must have observed, cut through meaningless generalities to the specific contributions Cukor made to his profession. His pattern is a good one to follow.

The *memorial* speech closely resembles the testimonial tribute except that the person or group honored is part of the past. That past, as a matter of fact, can be so far removed from the lives of those in the audience that if you were called upon for a memorial speech you would have to take pains to make the experience meaningful to those gathered. To speak in memory of one who means nothing to today's generation is pointless if the events of the past are not linked to those of the present. Lincoln, of course, made his famous memorial speech at Gettysburg while the terible war still raged. He would have used a different approach had he been speaking of the dead of the

---

[2] Charles Brackett delivered this tribute to his friend at a testimonial dinner given in Los Angeles by Delta Kappa Alpha, national cinema fraternity. The text was transcribed from the CBS Radio Pacific Network broadcast produced by your author, February 15, 1959. Used through the courtesy of Mrs. Charles Brackett.

War of 1812. The memorial address is perhaps the most difficult one in which to avoid the criticism, "Words, mere words."

Look for ties between the problems and events of the earlier days and those of the present. Show that those who went before were people, not institutions—or statues in the park. If possible, give current manifestations of their influence, as psychology professor Herman Harvey did in the beginning of a 1961 memorial tribute to Ethel Barrymore:

> Within the halls of the University of Southern California, a plan is beginning to assume shape and substance, a plan to assemble the many and diverse materials having to do with the American theatre and American drama, original sources which establish the historical facts of its people and its ideas—letters, books, scripts, films—each bringing into unique focus a particular fragment of this incredibly vital endeavor.
>
> This collection is intended as a living memorial to a woman who, in her time, became the very spirit and tradition of the theatre—Ethel Barrymore. Her enormous talent as an actress certainly had something to do with this tribute, but there was something more. The talent by itself would have gained her only a thin shell of fame which by now should be little more than an historical notation. Somehow the impression of the woman has remained, even grown in its effect and its extent, for there were also her qualities as a human being—a vigor, a vitality, a sparkling elegance. These as much as anything made it appropriate that there should be such tribute to Ethel Barrymore.[3]

The memorial tribute often coincides with a dedication of a building, a statue, a collection. If so, it may mean that a dedicatory message—to appear on a plaque, for instance—must be read to the audience. This message should be blended into the speech so that it doesn't dangle as a loose end in the ceremony. Certainly a speaker should not attempt to read it cold: The language is likely to be formal and complicated.

Obviously the tone of delivery in a tribute should be appropriate to the moment, especially if it is a *eulogy*, which is usually given at a

---

[3] The excerpt is from *Trojan Digest*, CBS Radio Pacific Network, October 1, 1961, as adapted from CBS Television's *Touch of Fame*, KNXT-CBS, August 13, 1961.

funeral service. Special consideration must be given to the fact that close relatives of the deceased will be present for the service. This caution applies to both tone and content. Some statements, though appropriate to a tribute after time has healed the wounds of grief, are simply too painful to loved ones a few days after the death. Surely, controversial matter should be avoided. A few years ago, with the family sitting at the graveside, the speaker at the burial service of a respected statesman saw fit to attack the former critics of the dead man instead of confining his remarks to the man about to be lowered into the ground. It was a jarring note that brought no comfort to those there to say farewell to a great man whose critics had long been forgotten. A much more tactful and gracious handling of the criticism which all public men receive is found in President Richard Nixon's eulogy of a former President:

> People often disagreed with Dwight Eisenhower, but almost nobody ever hated him. And I think this was because he himself was a man who did not know how to hate. Oh, he could be aroused by a cause, but he could not hate a person. He could disagree strongly—even passionately, but never personally. When people disagreed with him, he never thought of them as enemies, he simply thought, "Well, they don't agree with me."
>
> I remember, time after time when critics of one sort or another were misrepresenting him, or reviling him, he would sit back in his chair, with that wonderful half-smile, half-frown. He'd say: "I'm puzzled by those fellows."
>
> And he was genuinely puzzled by frenzy and by hate. Because he was incapable of it himself, he could never quite understand it in others. The last time I saw him, that was what he talked about. He was puzzled by the hatreds he had seen in our times. And he said the thing the world needs most today is understanding, an ability to see the other person's point of view, and not to hate him because he disagrees.
>
> That was Dwight Eisenhower.[4]

A note on style: More than any of the other speeches of courtesy, speeches of tribute approach the poetic in compositional style. The sentiments are more nobly phrased, the phrases more carefully turned. In the settings at which they are delivered this formal style is ac-

[4] *The Philadelphia Bulletin,* March 31, 1969.

cepted—as it probably would not be in the ordinary introductory or welcome speech, where formality would appear to be pomposity. Naturally, highblown or empty phraseology is out of place anywhere. But you can, since it is customary to read such speeches, be more literary in speeches of tribute than you can be in most other situations. Time, however, will alter how far a speaker can go, as we can see from these opening lines of Robert G. Ingersoll, spoken at the funeral of his brother Ebon in 1879:

> Dear Friends, I am going to do that which the dead oft promised he would do for me.
>
> The loved and loving brother, husband, father, friend, died where manhood's morning almost touches noon, and while the shadows still were falling toward the west.
>
> He had not passed on life's highway the stone that marks the highest point. . . . While yet in love with life and raptured with the world, he passed to silence and pathetic dust.
>
> Yet, after all, it may be best, just in the happiest, sunniest hour of all the voyage, while eager winds are kissing every sail, to dash against the unseen rock, and in an instant hear the billows roar above a sunken ship. For whether in mid sea or 'mong the breakers of the farther shore, a wreck at last must mark the end of each and all. And every life, no matter if its every hour is rich with love and every moment jeweled with joy, will, at its close, become a tragedy as sad and deep and dark as can be woven of the warp and woof of mystery and death.

And, a little later:

> Life is a narrow vale between the cold and barren peaks of two eternities. We strive to look beyond the heights. We cry aloud, and the only answer is the echo of our wailing cry. From the voiceless lips of the unreplying dead there comes no word; but in the night of death hope sees a star and listening love can hear the rustle of a wing. . . .[5]

Simpler in phrasing—it was delivered impromptu at a Quaker service—but rich in imagery was Adlai Stevenson's final farewell to a friend, Lloyd Lewis. It began:

[5] "A Tribute to Ebon C. Ingersoll," *The Works of Robert G. Ingersoll* (New York: The Dresden Publishing Co., 1902), XII, 389-90.

I have been asked to share in these farewells to a friend.

I think it is a good day for this meeting. It is April now and all life is being renewed on the bank of this river that he loved so well. I think we will all be happy that it happened on this day, here by the river with the spring so clear, and the west wind so warm and fresh. I think we will all be the better for this day and this meeting together.[6]

Whether it is a speech of tribute you are preparing or an introduction of the local sheriff, if you are in doubt about style or tone or content, remember the question we urged you to consider in Chapter Two: "Why am I making this speech to this audience at this time?" Answer it and you won't stray from the proper approach to expressing courtesy—or any other message you wish to convey.

And so, dear reader, we have passed together through the forest and into the clearing. From this point you will travel without formal guide—though I hope you will keep this paper guide at hand to help you when you have need of another look at the road map. I wish you, expert that you now are, Godspeed, good speaking.

[6] Mr. Stevenson's impromptu remarks at Libertyville, Illinois, April 23, 1949, were transcribed by a public stenographer, asked to make a record of the Quaker service by Mrs. Louise Wright.

APPENDICES

Sample Outline Form

AUDIENCE: _____ DATE: _____

TOPIC: _____

OBJECTIVE: To _____

_____

_____

I. INTRODUCTION
   A. Attention Statement
   B. Interest Step
   C. Preview

II. BODY
   A. Point One
      1. Support for point one
         a. Supplemental material
         b. Supplemental material
      2. Further support for point one
         a. Supplemental material
         b. Supplemental material

B. Point Two (if any)
   1. Suport for point two
      a. Supplemental material
      b. Supplemental material
   2. Further support for point two
      a. Supplemental material
      b. Supplemental material

C. Point Three (if any)
   1. Support for point three
      a. Supplemental material
      b. Supplemental material
   2. Further support for point three
      a. Supplemental material
      b. Supplemental material

III. CONCLUSION

A. Summary
B. Thesis (stated or implied)
C. Quotation, illustration, challenge

Speech Report Form

Your name————————————

Section———— Instructor————————

I. *BASIC DATA*

Date of speech———— hour———— Occasion————————

Name of principal speaker————————————

II. *PHYSICAL DATA*

Place of speech————————————————

Physical problems of room, if any————————————

Accoustical conditions————————————

III. *AUDIENCE PROFILE*

Estimated size————

Activity level at outset: passive————; active————.

Attitude at outset: sympathetic_____; antagonistic_____; open-

minded_____.

Interest in subject: high_____; low_____; average_____.

Knowledge of subject area: layman's_____; specialist's_____.

Composition: (As applicable, give a brief description of audience in terms of age, sex, occupation, ethnic
background, socioeconomic status, and special
background or interest.)

IV. SPEAKER PROFILE

General appearance_____

Vocal performance_____

Effectiveness of delivery_____

V. CONTENT

Brief summary:

_____

_____

_____

Thesis:

_____

_____

VI. YOUR OVER-ALL REACTION

Index